'Wherever you look there will be advice – u[...] feed children. Jo Cormack offers somethin[g] important in *Helping Children Develop a Positive Relationship with Food*. She offers evidence and insight on the "how" of feeding children. As a health psychologist and someone who developed a negative relationship with food from a young age, I can vouch for the importance of the "how". If we are to tackle the obesity epidemic and, more importantly, build self-esteem and body confidence, we need to start working with young people from a very early age. Cormack provides many practical ways to provide this nurturance, offering creative solutions to eating problems in young children and embedding these solutions within the practice of early years professionals. Case studies bring the book to life, making it accessible and very user-friendly. While it is aimed at professionals, I would recommend it to parents too.'

– Dr Nicola Davies, health psychologist, counsellor and author

'As a pediatric dietitian working with families on a variety of feeding issues, I am so thrilled Jo's book is now available to help continue the hard work parents are doing at home, in primary care settings. Childcare providers have a unique opportunity to influence a child's relationship with food for life, and I hope to see this timely resource on the desk of each child-minder, preschool and nursery teacher in the UK and beyond.'

– Natalia Stasenko, MS, RD, Feeding Bytes

'The best part is that this book makes caring for children easier and more satisfying. Imagine an end to power struggles with children at the table. Imagine not having to nag or remind children to eat. Imagine mealtimes that are about connection and curiosity, instead of getting bites in. This book will show you how to make that a reality, and children will eat better for it. It's a win-win.'

– Jenny McGlothlin, MS, CCC-SLP, author of
Helping Your Child with Extreme Picky Eating

'This book offers comprehensive guidance that will support the personal, social and emotional development of young children. Both early years professionals and parents would benefit from reading this.'

– Emma Bacon, author of Rebalancing Your Relationship with Food

of related interest

Nurturing Personal, Social and Emotional
Development in Early Childhood
A Practical Guide to Understanding Brain Development
and Young Children's Behaviour
Debbie Garvey
Foreword by Dr Suzanne Zeedyk
ISBN 978 1 78592 223 7
eISBN 978 1 78450 500 4

Promoting Young Children's Emotional Health and Wellbeing
A Practical Guide for Professionals and Parents
Sonia Mainstone-Cotton
ISBN 978 1 78592 054 7
eISBN 978 1 78450 311 6

Promoting Emotional Wellbeing in Early Years Staff
A Practical Guide for Looking after Yourself and Your Colleagues
Sonia Mainstone-Cotton
ISBN 978 1 78592 335 7
eISBN 978 1 78450 656 8

Developing Empathy in the Early Years
A Guide for Practitioners
Helen Garnett
ISBN 978 1 78592 143 8
eISBN 978 1 78450 418 2

Learning through Movement and Active Play in the Early Years
A Practical Resource for Professionals and Teachers
Tania Swift
ISBN 978 1 78592 085 1
eISBN 978 1 78450 346 8

Helping Children Develop a Positive Relationship with Food

A Practical Guide for Early Years Professionals

JO CORMACK

Jessica Kingsley *Publishers*
London and Philadelphia

First published in 2018
by Jessica Kingsley Publishers
73 Collier Street
London N1 9BE, UK
and
400 Market Street, Suite 400
Philadelphia, PA 19106, USA

www.jkp.com

Library of Congress Cataloging in Publication Data
Names: Cormack, Jo, author.
Title: Helping children develop a positive relationship with food : a
    practical guide for early years professionals / Jo Cormack.
Description: London, UK ; Philadelphia : Jessica Kingsley Publishers, 2018. |
    Includes bibliographical references.
Identifiers: LCCN 2017036573 | ISBN 9781785922084 (alk. paper)
Subjects: LCSH: Children--Nutrition--Psychological aspects. | Food
    preferences in children. | Food habits--Psychological aspects.
Classification: LCC RJ231 .C67 2018 | DDC 613.2083--dc23 LC record available at
https://lccn.loc.gov/2017036573

British Library Cataloguing in Publication Data
A CIP catalogue record for this book is available from the British Library

ISBN 978 1 78592 208 4
eISBN 978 1 78450 486 1

Printed and bound by CPI Group (UK) Ltd, Croydon, CR0 4YY

Contents

Acknowledgements

Special thanks to Dr Patricia Mucavele (PhD, RNutr, FRSPH, OBE), Head of Nutrition, Children's Food Trust, for generously sharing her time and expertise to help me ensure that references to the Trust were accurate. Thanks also to Simone Emery and Louise Usher for their input on my chapters relating to oral motor skills and allergies. I am very fortunate to have the support of such knowledgeable and talented women. Thanks to Sarah Brand, an early years practitioner and SENCO, whose expertise and experience in early years I continue to learn from. Thanks to Andrew James at Jessica Kingsley Publishers, for his ongoing support and advice. And, finally, thanks to all the children and families I have had the privilege to work with and who have taught me so much.

INTRODUCTION

We eat several times a day, each and every day. Food is a huge part of our routine – in fact, our very lives depend on it! For most children, eating can be a pleasurable experience, or at least something they do without thinking too much about it. For others, food can be an extremely challenging and complex area.

BACKGROUND

I wrote this book with three key goals in mind: first, to offer an accessible overview of some important theoretical concepts relating to how children eat; second, to offer some guidance (relevant to all children) on best practice in relation to food in an early years context; and third, to serve as a guide for early years practitioners who wish to feel confident about how to support children who may have a problematic relationship with food, with a particular focus on picky eating.

Although the government has recognised that there is a problem in terms of what foods children are eating, historically the key focus has been on increasing fruit and vegetable consumption.[1] In recent years, there has also been an effort to reduce the amount of sugar in children's diets, driven by concerns about rising levels of childhood obesity.[2] However, while awareness has been raised regarding what constitutes a healthy diet, actually addressing underlying eating behaviours has proved more challenging.[3]

I am a therapist, feeding consultant and doctoral researcher (exploring picky eating) and my interest in children's eating is concerned with the psychological, behavioural and emotional aspects of food and feeding. I am not a dietitian and this book is not really about *what* to feed children, so much as *how*. Of course, nutrition is a big part of the picture, but there are other books and guidance documents available which provide information about nutrition in an early years context.

This book is for you if you want to know more about the psychology of children's eating and about how to help them enjoy a varied and healthy diet. It is also for you if you want to know more about how to help children in your care who may struggle with challenges like being overweight or picky eating. There is an emphasis on working with parents and carers and on meeting your obligations as set out in the Early Years Foundation Stage (EYFS) Framework.

A FRESH LOOK AT HOW WE FEED CHILDREN...

Many of the concepts in this book challenge cultural norms in relation to feeding children. I invite you to step back, take a look at the research and re-appraise some assumptions that you may hold. While academic research into how we feed children is a burgeoning area in the UK, this has not translated into practice, either in terms of parenting or in an educational context. In this book, I draw particularly on the work of American feeding specialists and academics and share some ideas which are better known across the pond.

This book is all about shifting the goal posts: moving from the short term aim of 'get food down child', to the longer term aim of 'foster a positive relationship with food'. There are so many reasons why we feel that getting children to eat should be our main priority. I attempt to unpick these and offer an evidence-based alternative.

HOW TO USE THIS BOOK

There is more than one way to use this book. You can read it from cover to cover and gain an in-depth understanding of how to help children develop a positive relationship with food. You can also use it as a reference, going straight to a chapter or section which is relevant for you at a particular time. This is especially true of Section 10, in which I look in detail at specific issues like autism spectrum disorder (ASD) and sensory processing in relation to eating. However, a word of caution: if you approach the book in this way, first read

Sections 1 and 2 where I introduce some very important concepts which are necessary to an understanding of the rest of the book.

WHO IS THIS BOOK FOR?

Whether you are a nursery assistant, childminder, teacher or nursery manager, I hope there will be something in this book which will be of value to you. Some aspects of it are quite theoretical, because I think it is important to understand the rationale and evidence base underpinning the practical suggestions I make. Where it is included, I have tried to express theory in an accessible and meaningful way. Conversely, other aspects of this book are very much grounded in day-to-day practice. If you are an early years practitioner and any part of your work involves feeding children, I have written this book for you.

THINGS TO BE AWARE OF WHEN READING THIS BOOK

- Where I use the term 'parent' or 'parents' this is shorthand for 'parents and carers'. I understand that many people who may not be a child's parent take on the parental role.

- In order to protect anonymity, the case studies (except the one in Section 11) are fictitious but draw on elements of real situations and experiences.

While much of the theory is relevant to all children, feeding babies and toddlers under two is not covered in this book. This is a specialist area requiring a separate focus.

A NOTE ABOUT THE CHILDREN'S FOOD TRUST

The Children's Food Trust has been responsible for some extremely important work in relation to children's health and wellbeing in the UK. At the time of writing, they have very sadly announced their closure. I refer to and recommend several of their resources in certain sections of this book. You can still read and download these on their website despite their closure, as they will continue to be available.

ALL ABOUT A GOOD RELATIONSHIP WITH FOOD

In the first section of this book, we will think about what constitutes a good relationship with food and why it is important. I will introduce you to some key concepts which are essential to an understanding of how to promote and support a positive relationship with food. The most important of these is self-regulation – an idea that we will be coming back to again and again as we think about how children eat and how to feed them. I will invite you to reflect on what our role is in relation to feeding children and will introduce you to American feeding expert, Ellyn Satter's 'division of responsibility' model, which proposes an answer to this question. Finally, we will explore the importance of exposure and variety in helping children develop a positive relationship with food.

Chapter 1

WHAT IS A POSITIVE RELATIONSHIP WITH FOOD AND WHY DOES IT MATTER?

WHAT EXACTLY IS A POSITIVE RELATIONSHIP WITH FOOD?

This is one of those apparently simple questions that is really quite difficult to answer. Like many things, we know it when we see it. If we spot a child eating lots of different, nourishing foods with enjoyment and gusto, we might want to say that they have a positive relationship with food. But can we define it? Can we get closer to describing what a positive relationship with food is all about, in order to help children move closer to attaining this lofty ideal?

NUTRITION

Nutrition is a key aspect of a positive relationship with food. Children need to be adequately nourished in order to fully engage with the curriculum and access all of the opportunities available to them in whatever setting they attend.

Most early years practitioners will be familiar with Maslow's hierarchy of needs.[1] Maslow argued that, before higher level needs can be met (like the need for belonging or for self-esteem) more basic needs (like the need to be safe) have to be addressed. He expressed this theory visually, as a pyramid. At the very base of Maslow's pyramid are our physiological needs. These are the things our bodies require in order to work properly.

Just as a child who has not had enough sleep, or a child who is unwell, cannot function at full capacity, a child who has a very poor diet is at a disadvantage. Of course, there are many reasons why children might not to be able to access a healthy diet (including socio-economic factors) but sometimes it might be their negative relationship with food that is preventing them from reaching their full potential.

VARIETY

A child who ate the same meal every day could be adequately nourished if that meal was balanced, but we would not necessarily want to say that they had a positive relationship with food. Being able to enjoy a varied diet is so important. Each child is at a different stage in terms of their relationship with food and it is normal for young children to be distrustful of the unfamiliar. However, supporting children to be curious about foods they have not seen or tried before, and giving them exposure to foods that are new to them, is an intrinsic part of helping them develop a positive relationship with food. We will be exploring this in Chapter 4.

OUTCOMES FOR CHILDREN

While early years is about so much more than academic outcomes, there is a lot of research evidence showing that children who are better nourished have more success academically.[2] In other words, well-nourished children do better at school. Children who lack a positive relationship with food will also struggle with some of the social and emotional aspects of life. Eating is such an important part of our daily lives; problems in this area can have a significant negative impact on children's wellbeing.

For example, a child who dislikes fruit may attend a setting where fruit is always offered as a mid-morning snack. That child may feel anxious in the build up to snack time. They may feel excluded and different from their peers. Perhaps they will act out and express some of these difficult feelings through negative behaviour, which may have repercussions of its own. There are many social and emotional consequences emerging from something as simple as a child not being able to eat fruit. Problems with eating ripple through multiple areas of a child's life, from learning, to sleeping, to their social interactions and beyond.

IT'S NOT JUST WHAT CHILDREN EAT, IT'S HOW!

The content of children's diets – the nutritional qualities and the variety – are of course very important. For a child to eat in a psychologically healthy way though, *how* they eat, rather than *what*, comes into play. Are they able to tune into their body's signals and eat because they are hungry, rather than because of the adults around them? This is something we will be looking at in more depth in the next chapter. Are they able to enjoy the social side of meals? Are they relaxed and happy when they eat? What role does food play in their life? How children feel about eating is so important, and the adults around them have a lot to do with that.

'A positive relationship with food' describes eating behaviours whereby children eat a varied diet, enabling them to be well nourished. They eat in response to their bodies' cues and they are able to enjoy and benefit from the social side of meals.

YOUR UNIQUE OPPORTUNITY

As an early years practitioner, you are uniquely placed to have a positive influence on how the children in your setting relate to food. You and your colleagues may well be providing them with more than one eating opportunity every single day they attend. Your setting could be the only place where many of the children ever get to interact with and experience certain foods. It could also be the only regular chance some children get to eat communally.

This opportunity comes with responsibilities; you owe it to the children in your care to make sure that you adopt evidence-based good practice. You also need to do your best to help instil in them a joyful and psychologically healthy approach to eating. You can do so much: through what you model, through working with parents and through understanding and adopting best practice.

Research shows that in early childhood, children's eating behaviours are not yet set in stone.[3] There is a window of opportunity for adults to help them develop a positive relationship with food and to learn positive eating habits.[4] It is also a critical time when it comes to the development of children's food preferences[5] and there is evidence that eating behaviours learnt at a young age can influence how a person eats later on in life.[6] Seize this opportunity with both hands, and help give the children in your care a gift that will last a lifetime.

────────────────────

Chapter 2

SELF-REGULATION

In recent years, it has become the norm for informed practitioners and parents to take a 'behavioural' approach to what children do. Put simply, we reward the behaviour we want to see more of and do the opposite with behaviour we wish to reduce. The reward might not be tangible; it could be a reward in terms of positive attention or praise.

This works well when we think of behaviours like tidying away toys. If we want a young child to pick up the bricks when they have finished playing with them, we might praise them when they do this or we might give them a sticker for their reward chart. Maybe we will reinforce that behaviour by smiling at the child and describing what a fantastic job they have done.

It is very easy to see how this behavioural approach gets used with eating. If a child eats 'well' or tries something new, they are often praised or even rewarded. Sometimes they are given stickers or 'clean plate awards'. However, this is based on the mistaken assumption that eating is a behaviour to be modified. In other words, we see eating as a behaviour that we want children to perform for us.

When we lump eating in with other things like tidying away or trying hard during phonics, we are in fact not helping children eat for the right reasons. What these 'right reasons' are will be explained in the section which follows. It all comes down to where the motivation to behave in a certain way comes from. Does it come from inside the child (intrinsic) or outside the child (extrinsic)? In fact, the benefit of extrinsic motivation for any kind of behaviour has been questioned,[1] but, for eating, it is clear cut. We need children to be eating because their bodies tell them to, rather than in response to the adults around them. Seeing eating as a bodily process, instead of a behaviour to be driven by adults, is the first step towards supporting a positive relationship with food.

Self-regulation is a term which is used in many different contexts.

When we talk about self-regulation in relation to eating, we are describing the process whereby we eat in response to signals from our body and brain (appetite) and we stop eating when our body tells us that we have had enough.

Influential American child feeding expert, Ellyn Satter, describes several things we need to be able to do in order to self-regulate effectively,[2] including:

- cope with hunger well enough to be able to eat in line with a socially accepted pattern of snacks and meals

- feel sure that there will be enough food available for us to eat at each meal and snack (and that this will include something we can enjoy)

- be able to eat in a conscious way, where we tune into our bodies' signals

- be able to stop eating when we have had enough.

Let's look a little more closely at each of these points.

COPING WITH HUNGER

From a young age, some children may have been raised to eat in a grazing pattern. This means that they have lots of small opportunities to eat and miss out on fully experiencing their natural appetite. It is true that children have small stomachs and need more eating opportunities than adults and older children. However, this has perhaps been taken too far and, based on my clinical experience, I would suggest that many children eat so frequently they have become divorced from their experiencing of hunger cues.

There are many reasons why this may happen. Sometimes children dictate when and what they eat; this is especially true for picky eaters when parents are anxious about their eating, thus giving the child a lot of control over their diet. Sometimes, parents use food as a means of behaviour management or entertainment. It is socially normal, for example, to give a child a packet of crisps as they go around the shops in a pushchair, or to give them some raisins on a car journey. This keeps the child busy but can also prevent them from learning to experience and interpret their physical cues.

Children who are hungry can behave in a way that is more challenging for parents too. It can be easier to avoid letting them get hungry in order to prevent this. Again, this interferes with appetite and self-regulation. One of the challenges when it comes to feeding children is walking the fine line between preventing them from experiencing their appetites and letting them get excessively hungry. We will explore this in Chapter 13 when we look at creating an ideal meal and snack schedule.

Another reason parents may over-protect children from hunger comes down to the question of how they perceive their role. Making sure a child is not hungry can be part of a person's sense of themselves as a nurturing parent. By the time a child comes to you, it may be the case that they have never really had the opportunity to experience hunger and fullness because of how they have been fed at home.

Of course, the kind of hunger that I am talking about in this context is appropriate, healthy hunger. It is part of the rhythm of the day; a child feels hungry before meals and full after them. This is very different from hunger born of neglect or deprivation, which is never acceptable. Good self-regulation is based on children feeling appropriately hungry before a snack or meal and feeling satiated (that they have had enough) once they have eaten.

Thinking about the children in your setting, the ability to cope with hunger is all about a child being able to experience the feelings we get when we are hungry (along with the thought that they would like something to eat) and then being able to tolerate those thoughts and feelings until the next scheduled snack or meal. This can be especially challenging for a child who has been over-protected from hunger at home.

FEELING SURE THAT THERE WILL BE ENOUGH ACCEPTABLE FOOD AVAILABLE

This factor can perhaps be better understood by looking at what happens when a child is not confident that there will be acceptable food available to them. For example, if a child knows that their snack at nursery will be some kind of fruit, but they do not like any fruit at all, they won't feel secure in the knowledge that they will be able to have something to eat at snack time. This causes anxiety, which has a very negative impact on eating. It can also make children feel socially excluded and different from their peers.

For some children, meals may be chaotic and inconsistent at home. Food poverty is sadly also a huge issue, and some children may simply not have that confidence that there is always going to be enough to eat. This insecurity hampers self-regulation because if we don't trust that there will always be enough good food available, we move towards eating for survival rather than eating in response to our bodies cues. It makes sense from an evolutionary perspective (thinking about the survival of the human race) that when food is scarce, if we come across something to eat, we should consume as much as we possibly can. This is very different from eating in response to physical cues.

It can be useful to recognise that some children who have experienced neglect or come from a background of socio-economic deprivation may find self-regulation especially hard. This is something that must be borne in mind when working with looked after or adopted children. Children who have experienced neglect may well have unusual ways of eating. Perhaps they have been used to meals and snacks happening at irregular, unpredictable times. Maybe they often experienced excessive hunger and their drive to eat overrides their ability to listen to their internal cues. Maybe they find it almost impossible to eat at a table with others. To learn more about how to support a positive relationship with food in this vulnerable group of children, read American feeding specialist, Dr Katja Rowell's excellent book *Love Me, Feed Me*.[3]

EATING IN A CONSCIOUS WAY

Mindful eating is an area which has experienced an increased level of interest recently. If we eat in a hurried or distracted way – with the television on, for example – it is very hard to listen to our internal signals. As a practitioner, you can foster an eating environment where you enable children to eat in a conscious way. You can model listening to your own bodily signals and interpreting and responding to them. This is something I talk more about in Chapter 19.

STOPPING EATING WHEN WE HAVE HAD ENOUGH

Recognising that feeling of being full, or 'satiety', is an essential aspect of a positive relationship with food. Given the focus on childhood obesity these days, it is easy to see why it is so important to help children learn to recognise when they are full up. Poor self-regulation has been recognised as a significant contributing factor to obesity.[4] When it comes to obesity management, it is frustrating that there is not more emphasis on boosting children's self-regulation skills, rather than focusing on adults restricting what children eat. This is a complex dynamic which we will be looking at in Chapter 38, all about childhood obesity.

Chapter 3

THE DIVISION OF RESPONSIBILITY MODEL

The 'division of responsibility' is an approach, better known in the USA than in the UK, which was developed by Ellyn Satter. The division of responsibility questions conventional ideas about an adult's 'job description' when it comes to feeding children. It is a very simple concept, but making it work requires a conscious and consistent effort.

In the previous chapter, we looked at some of Satter's work on self-regulation. Satter is a Registered Dietitian Nutritionist (RDN) and family therapist. This combination of skills and training coupled with many years of experience has perhaps helped her gain such valuable insights into the relational aspects of feeding. Giving children a positive relationship with food is about so much more than nutrition – Satter has a profound understanding of the emotional and behavioural dynamics which underpin children's eating.

Satter began writing her seminal book, *Child of Mine*[1] in 1979 and it is still a valued resource today. She has written several other books and has also produced a video and teacher's guide (see the Resources section). In *Child of Mine*, she sets out her philosophy.

With the division of responsibility:

> Parents are responsible for the *what, when* and *where* of feeding; children are responsible for the *how much* and *whether* of eating.[2]

In other words, parents set the structure, location and content of meals and children make their own decisions about how much to eat and, indeed, whether to eat at all. We can easily swap 'parents' for 'adults' to see how the division of responsibility has meaning in an early years context. At the heart of the division of responsibility is the notion of building a feeding relationship based on trust.

WHAT THE DIVISION OF RESPONSIBILITY IS NOT

Satter's approach can be misunderstood, by those who have not taken the time to really understand it, as a permissive approach to feeding children. At first glance, it may seem that if children are empowered to make their own eating decisions, anything goes; that they can eat what they like, when they like. In fact, this could not be further from the truth. The child eats according to the structure set by the adult (at a particular time, in a particular place) and eats what feels right to them, from within the context of the food the adult has provided. This is illustrated by the following examples:

Charlie's mum made him a snack of apple and cheese chunks. Charlie said he didn't want it, and would prefer crackers. So Charlie's mum brought him crackers, which he ate happily. This is Charlie making his own eating decisions, but it is not the division of responsibility. This is because Charlie has taken responsibility for the 'what'. With the division of responsibility, it would have been fine for Charlie to choose not to eat his apple and cheese. He is responsible for the 'whether'. He would not have been given an alternative though.

Yasmin usually ate lunch at midday. At 11.30 a.m., she told her nanny she was hungry and was ready for her lunch. Her nanny asked her what she wanted and Yasmin asked for a tuna sandwich. This is not the division of responsibility because Yasmin is taking over the adult's responsibility for the 'when' and the 'what'. If Yasmin's nanny had been using the division of responsibility, she could have explained calmly to Yasmin that lunch was at midday, which would be soon. She could have told her that she had planned cheese sandwiches with salad that day.

THE POWER OF THE DIVISION OF RESPONSIBILITY

There are many reasons why Satter's model is so effective. Here are what I consider to be some of the most significant benefits:

- If a child is anxious about food, it might feel that giving them choice and control in terms of content and timing is supportive of their eating. In fact, giving them power in this way seems to raise anxiety. When the adult takes responsibility for what food will be served when, this leaves children with room to be in control via their decisions about how much and whether to eat. This lowers anxiety.

- The division of responsibility is extremely supportive of self-regulation. When children are able to listen to their bodies and eat according to internal signals, they are developing a key aspect of a positive relationship with food.

- The division of responsibility contributes to a positive mealtime environment. When adults are not concerned with doing the child's job – with affecting decisions about how much and whether a child eats – they are able to relax.

- With the division of responsibility, the potential for mealtimes to be used as an arena for power play and control battles is reduced. If the adult is not invested in the child's eating decisions, the child can't use them as a way of taking power or striving for autonomy. We'll be looking at this in more detail in Chapter 7.

Let's consider the following scenario to see how the division of responsibility can work in an early years setting.

SUE'S STORY

Little Stars was a nursery with 28 children (aged three and above) in the Buttercup Room. There were four members of staff assigned to that room. Four meals a day were served to the children: breakfast, mid-morning snack, lunch and tea.

At their staff meeting, Sue, a nursery assistant in the Buttercup Room, raised a concern that mealtimes seemed fraught with negativity and felt very stressful. The way things were currently set up, all four staff in the room moved around the long table where the children ate, praising children who were eating their food and making clear demands of the children who were not. There was a culture of specifying what and how much a child should eat. For example, a staff member might say: 'Just eat one more carrot then you can finish!' or 'Mummy will want you to eat all of your fish fingers. If you don't, you'll be hungry. Two more bites please.'

Sue described to the nursery manager how she felt things were not right at mealtimes. The rest of the team agreed but could not put their finger on how they could improve the situation. The nursery manager decided to spend a week eating lunch in the Buttercup Room with the children to see if she could establish what the problem was.

This is what she observed. With four adults moving around the table, judging and instructing the children in relation to how they were eating, the atmosphere was almost oppressive. Staff were kind but firm – they were never raising their voices or speaking angrily, but children felt under pressure. Some children enjoyed meals and ate well most days, but others struggled and there would always be several children upset by the expectations placed upon them. This, in turn, added to a negative and stressful atmosphere.

The manager went away and read all she could find regarding how to help children develop a positive relationship with food. She came across the division of responsibility model and immediately saw how the roles had got muddled up at Little Stars. Her staff saw it as their responsibility to influence the children's eating decisions. They were taking control of the 'whether' and the 'how much'. The approach the staff had traditionally taken was a conventional one – it echoed social norms concerning how adults see their role in relation to children's eating. The staff had not been doing anything ostensibly wrong or inappropriate but, clearly, something needed to change.

The nursery manager shared what she had learned about the division of responsibility with her team. Over the next few weeks, with support from Sue and the rest of the staff in the Buttercup Room, the division of responsibility was implemented. Rather than patrolling the room, the children were split into four tables with a staff member sitting on each, eating with the children. Children were told that they could decide what and how much they ate, in the context of what was offered. At first, some children would ask staff how much they needed to eat, but they slowly started to understand and accept the new system.

Sue and her colleagues were amazed at the impact the division of responsibility had. The first thing they noticed was that the atmosphere was much more pleasant and relaxed, although the children often left food, as though they were testing out whether these new rules were genuine. Soon though, staff noticed that children were eating better across the board.

Please note: As described in the introduction, this case is for illustrative purposes only. Little Stars is a fictitious nursery, although the description of staff and children's behaviour is based on experience and anecdotal evidence. In Section 11, I share a genuine case study of a setting in New Zealand who have made the division of responsibility work for them.

- Chapter 4

VARIETY AND EXPOSURE

So far, we've explored several key ideas which are central to supporting the development of a positive relationship with food. We've looked at how the motivation to eat needs to be internal rather than external. You've been introduced to Satter's division of responsibility model, an approach that supports self-regulation. The next pieces of the puzzle are the twin concepts of 'variety' and 'exposure'.

VARIETY

When we talk about variety, we are thinking about children being offered a wide range of foods, rather than being stuck in a repeating pattern where they cycle through the same few meals and snacks. Research shows that the biggest predictor of whether a child will accept a food is if they have been offered it before.[1]

> We like what we learned to like as children, and we learned to like what was available.[2]

In another study,[3] researchers found that the wider the variety of fruit and vegetables parents purchased, the more willing children were to taste these fruit and vegetables.

While it seems obvious that by not offering children a certain food, we remove the possibility that they will eat that food, actually there is a more subtle aspect to this idea.

Let's think about the message we give when we offer a limited diet. For example, if every time a parent takes a child out for a meal in a restaurant, they order them a cheese and tomato pizza, this tells the child that cheese and tomato pizza is for them; it is safe and appropriate. It is 'what they have'. The chicken salad that mum is ordering is 'not for them'. Children cling to familiarity and routine because it makes them feel secure. In order to help children enjoy a positive relationship with food, we need to make it the norm for them to be served things they have never seen before.

To put this another way, if we can help them to expect a varied diet, novelty will become familiar. They will learn to expect the unexpected. Neophobia (fear of new foods) is relatively common in young children, usually becoming apparent between the ages of 12 and 24 months.[4] Offering a limited diet reinforces neophobia because it makes the unknown even more alien and scary. Imagine you are four years old and, every morning, you are offered a piece of buttered toast and a cup of milk. Then one day you are offered a slice of papaya instead. For many children, this would be really disconcerting. However, if you knew that every morning you would be offered three fresh fruits and vegetables that were never the same two days in a row, being offered papaya would feel normal and non-threatening, even if you had never seen it before.

It is very easy to stick with what works and serve children reliable favourites that you know will go down well. This requires less planning, it might be cheaper and it will almost certainly entail less food waste. But it doesn't support the development of a positive relationship with food. This touches on the question of what our goal is when we feed children. If our main aim is to serve food that will be eaten, then sticking to tried and tested food items will work well. If your aim is to help children learn to enjoy a varied diet, you need to ensure that the selection of food offered is so diverse that children learn to expect novelty.

EXPOSURE

'Exposure' is just a technical term for describing an instance when a child is offered a particular food. So, going back to our papaya example, if a child is offered papaya for a snack on Wednesday, that is one exposure. If they are offered it again on Friday, that is a second exposure, and so on.

The power of 'mere exposure' to alter children's food preferences is well established. From the earliest stages of life, experiences with flavour shape present and future preferences.[5]

These days, many people are familiar with this notion that children need multiple exposures to new foods in order to learn to accept them. However, researchers have different ideas about precisely how many exposures to new foods are needed. Of course, it will also vary from child to child. There is evidence that the number of necessary exposures changes as a child gets older, ranging from hardly any in infants, to five to ten in two-year-olds, to up to 15 in three- and four-year-olds.[6] Interestingly, researchers looking at mothers feeding their children found that, in contrast with the high number of exposures children require in order to accept a new food, participants in their study were giving up on a new food after fewer than three exposures.[7]

Rather than trying to monitor the number of exposures to new foods that you offer children in your setting, a common-sense philosophy is to stick to the general principle that you need to serve things time and again, in order to help children accept them. In fact, counting exposures can even be counterproductive, because it can contribute to a controlling approach to food which we will be looking at in the next section of this book.

It is important to remember that children often respond negatively to a new food as a default reaction. Young children are only just learning to be emotionally articulate. They might see something new in front of them and their initial reaction is one of caution or even anxiety. They can't understand and express that in the moment. Instead, they just say, 'yuk!' What they mean is, 'I don't know what that is! I'm not sure about that!'

The second time a child is exposed to a new food, that cautious reaction will be slightly less powerful. Rather than immediately drawing a conclusion like 'Jane doesn't like papaya', when you hear that 'yuk!' remember how many exposures a child needs to have before they feel secure with a new food. Of course, in line with the division of responsibility discussed in the last chapter, exposing a child to a new food does not mean making them taste it.

The goal of providing repeated exposures to a wide variety of foods should inform your approach to food in your setting.

The more limited a child's diet at home, the more significant a role the setting they attend can have in the formation of their relationship with food. For a child with a varied, balanced diet at home, also getting access to a wide range of foods at pre-school, nursery or at the childminder's is great. However, for a child with access to a very limited diet at home, getting valuable exposures to a diverse range of foods that they would not otherwise have experienced can be life-changing.

●●●●● ● SECTION 2 ●

UNDER PRESSURE

In the second section of this book, we will be building on the understanding of self-regulation gained in the first section. We will be looking specifically at controlling feeding practices: ways of approaching food and feeding which do not support self-regulation or a positive relationship with food. We will consider the role of attention and praise in relation to eating – another area (alongside a controlling feeding style) where conventional feeding practices may in fact be detrimental to a positive relationship with food. Finally, I will argue for the controversial (but evidence-based) idea that, when it comes to how much food children need, perhaps they know best.

Chapter 5

WHAT IS A CONTROLLING FEEDING STYLE?

We have looked at some of the principles which are central to good practice in relation to feeding children, but what about the other side of the coin? Sometimes, to truly embrace good practice, we need to know what bad practice looks like.

The phrase 'a controlling approach to feeding' sounds very negative. Most early years practitioners would not identify with it. However, when we scratch the surface it becomes clear that, in contemporary British culture, many of the ways we deal with food in relation to children are in fact controlling. Recognising this is not about blame or judgement. To perpetuate socially normal ways of doing things is entirely understandable. As parents and as professionals, we learn from those around us, continuing with old approaches until new evidence comes to light and we take on new attitudes.

Controlling approaches to feeding children have been linked to increased fussy eating in children.[1] (Restricting children's eating can also be controlling, but we will be exploring this later in the book, in relation to obesity.) Researchers have not agreed on a way of defining what counts as a 'controlling feeding practice'.[2] Sometimes the word 'coercion' is used. Sometimes, approaches which adults may characterise as gentle encouragement can be experienced as controlling. This is a label which covers a broad spectrum of behaviours.

At the heart of the kind of controlling feeding practices that we are considering here, is an adult pressurising a child to eat[3] rather than letting them make their own eating decisions. At one end of the scale, we find practices which no one would argue were ethical, such as force-feeding a child, or limiting their food intake in an extreme way. Both of these things would clearly be abusive. At the other end of the scale, we find practices which are recognisable to anyone who has spent time around children, for example, persuasion, incentivisation to eat or encouragement.

In order to understand why these latter approaches are potentially controlling, we need to think back to Chapter 3 where we looked at the division of responsibility model. If we are truly letting a child take control of their eating decisions (the 'how much' and the 'whether') we do not need to try and directly influence their eating. As soon as we try to persuade them to take 'just one more bite' we are stepping into the territory of external rather than internal motivation; we are being controlling and in turn, hampering their ability to self-regulate.

This might sound challenging – it can be very hard to stop doing things that you have done for years and that everyone around you is doing. It can feel uncomfortable and even wrong, at first. But if you recognise that the opposite to being controlling is being facilitative, not passive, this will help you understand how and why to make the shift. Avoiding a controlling feeding style is not about letting children eat what they like, when they like. Remember, the adult sets the structure and the content of meals. It is about helping children listen to their bodies and eat in response to their internal cues.

Here are some of the different ways in which we can inadvertently use a controlling feeding style:

- **Reasoning**: This is when we offer a rational explanation to a child about why they need to eat or try something. Perhaps we talk about energy, and how they should eat more lunch in order to have running-around-energy for later.

- **Nutrition**: Using nutrition as an argument for why a child should eat is a form of reasoning. We might tell a child that they need to finish their yoghurt so that their bones can grow big and strong, or that if they don't eat vegetables, they won't get enough vitamins.

You may be thinking that these two practices (reasoning and using nutrition-based arguments) are supportive of helping children meet Early Learning Goal 05 (ELG05). In the next section of the book where we focus on the Early Years Foundation Stage (EYFS) Framework, we will explore how to work towards ELG05 in a way that is supportive of a positive relationship with food.

- **Waste**: Persuading children to eat by talking about how some children don't have enough food, or by telling a child what a shame it will be to put their left-overs in the bin, are examples of the waste argument. There are lots of opportunities away from mealtimes to teach children about waste and the importance of appreciating what we have.

- **Encouragement**: This is quite a broad category, including mild prods, like 'Go on, you might like it!' or 'Just try a little bit…': anything that could be described as an attempt to gently persuade a child to eat.

- **Authority**: To use authority in this context means telling a child to eat because that is the rule: because they should. Instructions like 'Eat up!' would fall into this category, as would telling a child how much they need to eat before they may finish.

- **Emotional blackmail**: Emotional blackmail is happening when a child is made to feel bad about the impact their eating decisions may have on someone else. Perhaps they are told to eat so that the cook doesn't feel sad, or Mummy isn't disappointed. 'Eat it up for me' falls into this category, where a child is asked to do something because it will make the adult happy.

- **Negotiation**: This is when the adult and child arrive at (sometimes very complex!) deals involving how many bites of what needs to be eaten until they can get down or have pudding.

- **Bribery**: Sometimes adults become desperate for children to eat and will bribe them with toys, treat foods or experiences. This is less likely to be used in an early years setting than in the home.

- **Incentivisation**: There is a fine line between bribery and incentivisation. The key difference is that bribery is spontaneous and one-off, whereas incentivisation is a more thought out, consistent strategy, like using a reward chart. Both interfere with self-regulation as they involve an adult trying to persuade a child to eat.

- **Threats or sanctions**: This is where a child is told they will miss out on something if they don't eat. For example, they might not be allowed a privilege that other children are allowed. Their eating is framed as 'bad behaviour'.

- **Comparison**: Children are often compared to their peers, and differences in their eating are highlighted in an attempt to motivate them to eat. For example, 'Lauren has finished all of hers!'

- **Entertainment**: Sometimes, adults use fun as a way of getting a child to eat. They might play games with the spoon; they might make broccoli into forests and persuade a child to 'nibble a tree'.

- **Intervention**: This is a physical approach to feeding where an adult would get involved with a child's eating by perhaps loading up their fork or even feeding them. Of course, feeding an infant or a child with special educational needs or disability (SEND) may be appropriate. This is not the case with a child who is developmentally capable of feeding themselves. Equally, to help a child in an age-appropriate way (e.g. cutting up a three-year-old's meat) is not controlling. However, spooning yoghurt into a child's mouth because they have decided they have had enough certainly is.

- **PR**: Food PR is a term I use to describe what happens when we 'hype up' certain foods by talking about how amazing they are; how delicious and good for us. Maybe we talk about ourselves, saying how much we love to eat them. Be careful to distinguish authentic enthusiasm about food from using food PR as a means of persuading a child to eat.

- **Withholding dessert**: This is an extremely common and socially condoned controlling feeding practice. Applying pressure on a child to eat by telling them that they can't have pudding is quite simply bad practice. Distinguished Professor and director of the Center for Childhood Obesity Research,[4] Leann Birch, found that rewarding children for eating a certain food increases their dislike of that food.[5] Similarly, making one food conditional on another significantly increases children's liking of the reward food.[6] By making pudding conditional on eating the main course, the long-term result is that the child will like pudding even more and the disliked food even less!

This list is not exhaustive and there are many, many things we do to encourage children to eat. They all have one thing in common though; they are about trying to influence a child's eating decisions in one way or another. In the next chapter, we will be exploring why this is a problem.

Chapter 6

WHY IS BEING CONTROLLING UNHELPFUL?

A controlling feeding style is unhelpful for many reasons. As we have seen, it gets in the way of self-regulation because eating becomes externally rather than internally motivated. It also gives children an incentive to use their eating behaviour as a means of getting attention or testing boundaries – something we will be looking at in the next chapter. For children who may be overweight, controlling feeding practices can also be extremely negative. In this chapter, we will be exploring what can happen for some children, when we use controlling approaches to feeding.

ANXIETY

Recent research[1] shows that there is a link between anxiety and picky eating, especially where eating is extremely limited. A child who is not accessing a varied diet and is very cautious about trying new foods, may well have a genuine anxiety response to those foods. Even the most gentle persuasion can be experienced by a child as pressure to eat and, as we explored in the last chapter, there is lots of research showing that pressure to eat can make eating worse.[2,3] If a child feels anxious because they are under pressure to eat, this is likely to make them feel an even greater need to take control themselves. In other words, if a child feels out of control because an adult is trying to persuade them to eat, this may cause them to dig their heels in further in order to manage their anxiety. Choosing not to eat becomes a coping mechanism.

When we are feeling anxious, we experience this physically as well as psychologically. For example, we might sweat, breathe more shallowly and have an increased heart rate. Anxiety also affects our digestive system and tells our body to stop bothering with food. This makes sense if we remember that we were hardwired for anxiety back in our cave-dwelling days. Our 'fight or flight' response enables us to instinctively react to a dangerous stimulus, by getting us ready to run or fight for our lives. If we are running from a sabre-toothed tiger, we are going to abandon our meal along with our digestive processes!

For a child who is worried about eating unfamiliar or disliked foods, pressuring them to eat and making them feel even more anxious is about the worst thing we can possibly do. It makes them more likely to feel a need to take control themselves (and refuse to eat) whilst interrupting their natural appetite and digestion.

RYAN'S STORY

Ryan is a four-year-old attending nursery. He is a very cautious eater. Eating aside, he is cautious by nature and takes a long time to settle most mornings, after his dad has dropped him off. Ryan has breakfast at nursery and he always struggles to eat much. His key worker, Farah, wondered if this was because he was always so unsettled at the beginning of the day.

One morning, Farah decided to sit with Ryan and persuade him to eat his toast. She used the biscuit cutters to cut it into dinosaur shapes for him, she 'walked' the dinosaurs around his plate and hopped them up to his mouth, hoping that her playful approach would induce Ryan to eat. Farah knew from experience that Ryan would be lethargic, and even less resilient than usual, if he didn't eat any breakfast.

Ryan just turned his head away, so Farah tried a different approach. She explained to Ryan that he needed his toast to have energy for the day. Feeling increasingly frustrated, she pointed out the other girls and boys, happily enjoying their toast. Nothing worked. Ryan got down crying and Farah felt despondent.

What had in fact happened was this: Ryan was upset as he found mornings hard. He wasn't a huge fan of toast and his separation anxiety was having a negative impact on his appetite. He felt very out of control. The only thing that Ryan could control in that situation was his eating. So he chose not to eat.

Farah's entire focus during breakfast was on Ryan. She was very close to him and directed all her attention towards him. Even without the controlling feeding approaches that Farah inadvertently used, Ryan would have experienced this intense focus on his eating as pressure. Although Farah was being kind and her intentions were good, she had made Ryan's eating worse.

WHAT COULD FARAH HAVE DONE DIFFERENTLY?

If Farah had been familiar with Satter's division of responsibility (see Chapter 3), she would not have felt the need to try to influence whether Ryan ate his toast. This would have freed her up to put her energy into creating a calm and positive eating environment. She could have sat down at the table as she did but, instead, directed her attention towards all the children, maybe engaging them with some calm conversation about the day ahead. What Ryan needed was to feel that he was in control – that he had the power to decide whether he ate his toast or not.

Had he been able to feel that way, he might have relaxed into the social interaction with Farah and the other children. The more relaxed he is, the more likely he will be to eat. This is a real paradox.

> The harder we try to get children to eat, the worse their eating will become. The more in control and relaxed children feel, the better their eating will be.

A NOTE ON THE 'CLEAN PLATE AWARD...'

Children are given stickers for eating well in many settings. Often, they even receive a sticker or certificate for finishing everything on their plate. This is detrimental to their relationship with food. It is easy to see why this is, now that we've looked in detail at self-regulation: a child shouldn't eat everything on their plate if their internal cues do not direct them to do so. To teach them to override their natural appetite in order to get a sticker is setting them up to be at a greater risk of obesity. I would like to see the end of the clean plate award in UK settings, because the research evidence is so compelling. Practitioners need to be made aware that it is an old-fashioned and ill-informed practice.

Chapter 7

ATTENTION AND PRAISE

Young children thrive on attention, and are programmed to seek it to such a degree that they even prefer negative attention to no attention at all.[1] To understand why this is relevant to good practice in relation to food, let's look briefly at where children are developmentally, during the toddler and pre-school years.

Early years is an exciting part of childhood, when children are learning rapidly and are full of curiosity and fun. It can be a challenging stage too! This phase is all about boundary testing, experimenting with autonomy and learning about how people react to one another. Although every child is unique, there are two strong urges that most children in this age bracket have in common: the need to learn and the need to feel safe.

Let's think about safety first. Once children are mobile and see themselves as separate individuals, they begin to wonder who is in charge and where the limits of their power are. In other words, they look for boundaries. A child living with clear and consistent boundaries will feel safe. We have all experienced what happens when a child comes up against a boundary they didn't know was there…they test it to see if it is real. And if it turns out not to be real – because the adult is not consistent or changes their mind – they push some more, to find out where it really is. Young children's boundary testing might look like 'bad behaviour' but really it is often about a need for security.

You only need to stop and watch a toddler or pre-schooler play for a little while, to witness their powerful drive to learn. They are finding out about the world around them and they are experimenting with what they can make happen. Sometimes, their ambitions outstrip their abilities and they end up feeling frustrated. They want to be independent, trying to do things all by themselves. They experiment with their personal power, saying 'No!' and testing what happens when they assert their autonomy.

Let's look at how these three things – boundary testing, attention-seeking and experimenting with autonomy – can come into play during mealtimes. There are many developmentally normal reasons why a young child might reject food (we will be looking at these in detail in Section 9). Maybe they are just seeing what happens, out of pure curiosity. Perhaps they want to see if the adult reacts with drama or emotion; this is exciting for a young child. Maybe they are simply asserting their independence. It is important to recognise that toddlers and pre-schoolers sometimes reject food just because of the age and stage they are at. If a child is getting a lot of attention for rejecting foods, this can paradoxically encourage them to repeat the behaviour because of the response it gets.

Positive attention is problematic too. If children get a lot of positive attention for eating well, this makes them see it as a behaviour that adults want from them. As discussed previously, this interrupts self-regulation. Equally, when we communicate a clear message that we want a child to eat (whether explicitly or through positive attention and praise) we are letting them know that, if they want to test a boundary and assert their independence, doing this through their eating is likely to be extremely effective.

PRAISE

'Catching children being good' and using praise is a cornerstone of modern practice in early years. It is second nature to praise the behaviour we want to see and to ignore or give sanctions for the behaviour we do not wish to see. Moving away from a praise mindset is one of the hardest things to get used to when you have decided that you will no longer give attention to children in response to their eating decisions.

Even sophisticated praise – praise which describes the behaviour rather than the child – is problematic in relation to food. It all comes back to why we want the child to be eating: because we want them to, or because their bodies want them to? Poor self-regulation in relation to eating has been linked to issues such as obesity, eating disorders and picky eating. The moment we equate eating with behaviours like tidying away or sitting nicely on the carpet, we are taking children further from their natural ability to self-regulate.

In the interests of balance, it is important to acknowledge that some researchers[2] have had success using praise and reward-based feeding strategies with children. Praise is also often used in the context of feeding therapy. In my experience, however, praising children for trying a new food in the context of mealtimes is problematic. I am concerned about the long-term outcomes of using praise, regarding both self-regulation and the likelihood of a child using their eating decisions to provoke a reaction in (or get attention from) adults.

In my clinical work with picky eaters, I have seen just how powerful resisting using praise can be. When parents stop praising children for eating, this seems to be an important aspect of taking the pressure off children in relation to how they eat. This reduction in pressure and focus frees children up to relax, enjoy meals and learn to self-regulate.

Although some professionals and feeding researchers do recommend the use of praise, many don't. For example, in their book for parents, US feeding experts Katja Rowell and Jenny McGlothlin[3] write:

> It may seem counterintuitive, but try *not praising* your child's eating even if she makes progress. Praising her today communicates that if she doesn't feel brave tomorrow, she has disappointed you. Praise can be another form of pressure. Children do best relying on *internal motivation* to eat, rather than eating for approval.

It is hard to make a change to a strategy that has been used for a long time, without putting something in its place. Here are some ways to give positive attention to children during mealtimes which don't interfere with their ability to self-regulate:

- If a child is eating something enthusiastically, describe this in a way that is free of value judgements:

  Instead of 'Well done for eating your peas, Jerome!'

  Try 'Wow, Jerome, you look like you're enjoying those peas!'

- You don't need to ignore the fact that children are eating a meal or snack; you can focus on the sensory qualities of the food:

  'Karen, that carrot stick looks crunchy! What kind of noise does it make when you chew it?'

- Use the language of self-regulation:

  Instead of 'Are you sure you don't want your apple, Ahmed?'

  Try 'Is your tummy telling you that you have had enough to eat, Ahmed?'

JACK'S STORY

Jack was three years old when he started going to his childminder, Jane. His parents told Jane that Jack was a poor eater and the only way they could get him to eat anything was with a lot of praise and rewards on his star chart. Jane wasn't sure this was an approach that would work for her, because she understood about children's need to self-regulate. She worked hard at creating a relaxed eating environment without too much focus on children's eating. She explained her philosophy to Jack's parents, who were open minded and said they would be interested to see how Jack got on.

On his first day at Jane's, Jack took one look at the bowl of pasta salad that Jane had served and said he didn't like it and wasn't going to eat it. 'Okay,' said Jane. 'You don't have to eat it if you don't want to. Just sit at the table while everyone else eats.' Jack was confused. He started throwing his pasta on the floor and shouting that he hated it. This behaviour continued at mealtimes for the next three days, and Jane reacted calmly and patiently, reiterating the message that Jack didn't have to eat anything he didn't like, but needed to sit at the table and be part of the meal.

On his second week, Jack understood how meals and snacks worked at Jane's. Jane made sure she always included something Jack's parents had said he was usually happy to eat, and Jane made it clear that Jack was in charge of his own eating decisions. She had expectations about his behaviour, but not about what and how much he ate. Slowly, he stopped using his eating decisions as a way of getting attention, for one very simple reason: it didn't work. Jane kept the children engaged in relaxed conversation and slowly, Jack began to eat better and better. Jane was able to share her approach with Jack's parents so that the same messages were reinforced at home.

Chapter 8

WHO KNOWS BEST?
Learning to trust children

If we are committed to an approach to feeding children that gives them space to make their own eating decisions, we need to trust that they know what they need. Remember, this is in the context of the varied and healthy foods that we are providing for them. There is a fundamental problem with the opposite view: the view that we are the best judges of what children need. The reason for this is that during the toddler and pre-school years, children's needs for nutrients and energy fluctuate greatly.

When we are calculating how much food to prepare for children, of course we need to think of their age and stage and recommended portion sizes. However, guidelines on portion are precisely what it says on the proverbial tin; they are a guide. While we can make generalisations about what an average active four-year-old may need to consume in a day, we can't know exactly what the four-year-old in front of us needs on this particular day.

As adults, our need for food is fairly constant, barring dramatic changes in our energy output. We make the assumption that children are the same, but this is simply not the case. We also often assume that children need more and more food as they get older. Again, this is not necessarily the case. Children may need to eat a lot during rapid phases of growth and then less as their growth slows.

A characteristic of toddlerhood is fluctuating appetite.[1] To better appreciate this, let's consider what scientists[2] say about how a child grows in the first few years of life:

During the first year of life, an average infant gains 7 kg in weight and 21 cm in length. During the second year of life, growth is about 2.3 kg and 12 cm, with most toddlers reaching an average weight of 12.3 kg and a height of 87 cm at two years of age. Between two and five years of age, weight gain slows down. Most children gain 1 kg to 2 kg and 6 cm to 8 cm per year. During this period, most toddlers and preschoolers experience a decrease in their appetite.[3]

A child who is growing rapidly may need lots to eat. That child's needs may be very different a few months later. The same authors also point out that children may need less to eat than their peers if they have a smaller build. Equally, we have all met adults who remain slim despite always eating lots of food, just as other adults don't eat very much at all, and yet have a tendency to put on weight. We are all different, with differing bodies and metabolisms. Children are no exception.

Given that we will never correctly second-guess exactly what a child needs to eat on a given day, what are we left with? The answer is, we are left with trusting them to know best. And research tells us that they do know; children are excellent at eating just what they need. A fascinating experiment[4] looking at children aged between three and five years, involved the children being given puddings to eat. Some of the children were given a high calorie pudding, some were given a pudding that was lower in calories. After they had eaten the puddings, they were given free access to snacks (cookies and crackers). Most of the children who had eaten the lower calorie puddings unconsciously compensated for this by eating more of the snacks.

When we decide that we know best, that we think children ought to take 'just one more mouthful', we are telling them to override this natural ability to self-regulate and are increasing their risk of obesity. This is an intrinsic part of the 'get food down child' mindset – the notion that in order to be nurturing and do the right thing by the children in our care, we ought to get them to consume the amount of healthy food that we judge to be necessary.

If a child is not eating much at all and you find yourself feeling concerned about them (or if they seem to be eating too much and you are worried about their weight), look at them, not at what is on their plate. A child whose weight and growth are on track, who is active, energetic, alert and happy, is likely to be getting the right amount to eat. Persuading them to eat more (or less) than they naturally want to is seriously misplaced and will have a negative impact on their relationship with food.

If you are worried about a child, recommend that parents contact their child's health visitor or make a referral to the school nurse. These professionals can check a child's weight and growth. If they have further concerns, a child can be referred to their GP and on to a dietitian for assessment. If a child seems healthy and active, it is impossible for you to know that they have 'had enough' or 'not had enough' at any particular meal.

It is important to see the big picture. What has a child had to eat over the course of a whole day, or even a whole week? If we get too caught up with what happens at individual meals, we can hamper children's ability to self-regulate. If a child is overweight, we might do this by restricting. If we try to control how much a picky eater eats, this also exacerbates the issue. Portion sizes are a useful guide – use them when you consider quantities to serve and prepare, but then allow children to self-regulate by making their own decisions about what they actually eat.

FOOD AND FEELINGS

In this section, we will explore the concept of emotional eating and think about what this means for children. We will look at what happens when we reward or punish with food and will consider the language we use about our food and our bodies. Finally, I explain the importance of understanding your own relationship with food and how this can impact professional practice.

Chapter 9

UNDERSTANDING EMOTIONAL EATING

In this chapter and the next, we will be looking at 'comfort' or 'emotional' eating. This is where food is given emotional significance or eating takes on a function which is related to feelings. We'll be thinking about how children's early interactions with food can lead to a dysfunctional relationship with it later in life, and what implications this may have for your practice.

Emotional eating can be defined as eating in response to negative feelings, as a way of coping with those feelings.[1] These could be emotions such as sadness, anger, shame, anxiety or loneliness. You may be wondering how this could be relevant in an early years setting. On the whole, children do not have complete control over what and when they eat, so they are unlikely to turn to food as a coping mechanism during their time at pre-school or nursery. They are also not quite at an age when emotional eating usually begins to manifest itself.

Researchers looking at emotional eating found that the five- to seven-year-olds in their experiment significantly increased their calorific intake in response to stress.[2] However, they explain that toddlers tend to respond to stress by under-eating rather than over-eating. Thinking about emotional eating is relevant to children in early years settings because patterns established early on in life could potentially have an impact as a child gets older, even if the behaviours themselves are not yet evident.

An important concept – central to emotional eating – is loss of control. This means eating without being able to stop. Loss of control in relation to eating has been linked by researchers to obesity[3] in children and adults alike. Equally, studies show that food-related loss of control is significantly related to depressive and anxious symptoms in children. Scientists believe that some children are distracted and comforted by eating and that this helps them cope with difficult feelings.[4]

Another worrying outcome associated with emotional eating is the increased likelihood of eating disorders.[5] This makes sense when we think of a psychologically healthy relationship as being characterised by an awareness of physical cues followed by eating in response to them. Some interesting research[6] points to mindfulness as a promising treatment approach for eating disorders (and obesity). This is partly attributed to how mindfulness supports 'self-regulation and the body's growing capacity to observe its internal state'.[7] Of course, eating disorders are extremely complex and have many contributing factors, including social considerations and family factors. Self-regulation is not the whole story, but it is an important part of it.

WHAT CAN YOU DO TO HELP PREVENT EMOTIONAL EATING?

Pay attention to reports from parents, of emotional or uncontrolled eating

This could signal that a child is struggling to cope with difficult feelings. Research shows that this is especially true of anxiety.[8] Understand these kinds of behaviours as red flags which can help draw your attention to underlying emotional problems.

Help children learn to allow themselves to experience difficult feelings

We all have emotions that can be tricky. If you stop to think about how hard it can be for an adult to experience rather than avoid a troubling feeling, just think how hard it is for a child. Emotional eating is all about avoiding those feelings. You can help children practise accepting and feeling their emotions, by giving them messages that it is okay to be sad, it is okay to be worried and we all feel this way sometimes.

Give children vocabulary to name bodily sensations

This is the precursor to helping them become emotionally articulate (see the next point). Children need to be able to sense feelings before they can name them. Start teaching these skills by helping them describe physical sensations like feeling hot, full, sweaty or tired.

Give children the words for their difficult feelings

A huge part of accepting and expressing feelings is concerned with language. That's why experiencing troubling emotions can be especially hard for a child whose language skills are not very developed. If a child exhibits a certain feeling, tell them 'you feel sad' or 'you feel cross'. For younger children, do this in the third person: 'Ayesha feels frustrated!' Naming their feelings for them is an important step towards helping children do this for themselves.

Model the acceptance of difficult feelings

Show the children in your setting that we all feel bad sometimes and we can accept, acknowledge and share this: 'Mrs Green is feeling a bit sad today. She's going to sit quietly and think about her tricky feeling and then maybe have a chat to Mr Jones, because talking always helps.'

Chapter 10

REWARDING AND PUNISHING WITH FOOD

This chapter is a continuation of the previous one in that it builds on the important concept of keeping food and feelings separate. As we've seen, emotional eating happens when food is used as a way of coping with tricky feelings. We can help children avoid this way of eating by teaching them psychologically healthy, constructive ways of dealing with their emotions. We can also help prevent children using 'treat food' to manage their feelings by being mindful of the emotional significance we give to food.

We give food emotional significance in the following ways:

- rewarding with food

- punishing with food

- incentivising with food

- withholding dessert

- how we talk about food.

Let's take a closer look at the first three things in this list. The next chapter is dedicated to how we talk about food so we'll be exploring that in some depth later. We have already touched on withholding dessert in Chapter 5.

REWARDING WITH FOOD

In our culture, rewarding or incentivising with food is standard practice. In some (but not all) early years settings, sweets are given to children to celebrate good behaviour or recognise an achievement. Not only does this further raise the pedestal treat foods are already perching upon, it also creates a strong association in children's minds: 'I am approved of, I am given sweet foods.' It is not difficult to see how this can be internalised so that when that child grows up and is feeling a little low on self-esteem, they can get some of those good feelings of being approved of by eating something sweet. Really, this is tantamount to equating food and love. It gives food an emotional currency.

The health content of the reward food is not the most important factor here. It would also be problematic if a child were to be rewarded with some carrot sticks for good behaviour. Self-regulation is key. If a child is given food because they have done something well, this is not supportive of teaching them to eat in response to their body's cues. It brings us back to children eating for external rather than internal reasons.

Although we immediately think of over-eating being the main challenge connected to emotional eating, research with three- to six-year-olds has shown that when parents use food as a reward, or in an emotional way, this correlates with under-eating too.[1] There is no scenario where using food as a reward is a good idea.

If you have decided to recognise children's achievements in a material way (in other words, by giving them something) there are lots of ways to do this without turning to food. Here are a few ideas:

- Let them sit in a special chair or on a special cushion for the day. They will be very proud of the elevated status this gives them.

- Let them choose a non-food prize, such as a notebook or some colouring pencils.

- Let them be the first in the line when they go out to play or when they go home at the end of the session.

- Give them a special job, like being snack monitor that day.

- Let them take home a special 'great behaviour teddy' for the night.

There are so many creative ways to recognise good behaviour which do not involve anything edible. You probably already use many of them. It is good practice to have a clear and consistent system which children can understand and engage with. If you are in the habit of giving edible rewards or incentives, think about coming up with a new system that does not use these.

Should there be a blanket ban on 'treat food' in your setting?

Balance is key, and being too puritanical or restrictive is never a good idea. For example, I would argue that there is nothing wrong with giving children a small amount of chocolate as part of a special occasion. You may be wondering why this is alright when giving a child a lolly because they have done well in a spelling test is not alright. It all comes down to what message has been communicated.

If we give a child some chocolate because it is Christmas or Diwali, this is not conditional on their behaviour. The message is, 'let's celebrate!' Eating can be a joyful and celebratory experience and that is a psychologically healthy phenomenon. However, if a child is given some chocolate because they tidied up the bricks without being asked, the message is, 'You are a good person and I approve of you'. This is entirely conditional on the child's behaviour and therefore feeds into an association of food with feelings about the self.

The decision about whether or not to have a blanket ban on sweets, chocolate and so on is one for each setting to make for itself. My advice is to consider your policy carefully (see Chapter 22). Apply your policy consistently and, if you do decide to allow treat foods to be shared with children in certain circumstances, make sure they are never given as a reward.

PUNISHING WITH FOOD

In current practice, talk of 'punishments' is seen as very old-fashioned. Usually, the term 'sanctions' is used. Expressing disapproval through food is unhelpful, however we dress it up. It is the other side of the 'food reward' coin. When we say to a child, 'You can't have a sweet like the rest of the group, because you kicked Johnny', we are communicating that same association between treat food and approval, even though it is through the absence rather than the presence of the treat. Anecdotal evidence suggests that, just as using food to manage behaviour is common practice among parents in our culture, it is also sometimes used by childminders. It is easy to see how this is less likely to be the case in more formal settings like pre-schools and nurseries.

INCENTIVISING WITH FOOD

The most common scenario where food is used to manage behaviour would seem to be incentivising with food. Again, this is more usual in less formal settings which mimic the home, like at the childminder's house. The following example illustrates why this is such a tempting practice.

LACEY'S STORY

Lacey was three years old and her childminder was working with her parents to help her learn to use the potty. Lacey's mum felt that Lacey should already be toilet trained at her age and there was a bit of anxiety around this. She asked Lacey's childminder to help (Lacey attended three days a week) and the childminder was happy to do so.

Lacey's childminder started giving Lacey a sweet every time she successfully used the potty. It seemed to be working; Lacey was learning fast and felt very positive about using the potty. She was always very proud of herself when she got her sweetie and would ask for it as soon as she sat on the potty.

This is a clear example of the argument that just because something works, that doesn't necessarily mean it's a good idea. This approach to teaching new behaviours is what psychologists call 'operant conditioning'. It involves repeatedly providing a positive consequence (a reward) for an action so that the recipient learns to expect the reward and to associate the behaviour with the pleasure of getting the reward. The person is then more likely to repeat that behaviour in the future.

Operant conditioning is very powerful. A child like Lacey who learns that using the potty results in getting a sweet will probably be keen to use her new found skills! But consider the message that Lacey is getting: 'I approve of you, here is a sugary treat.' Earlier in this section of the book, we explored just how dangerous this message can be. It is better that Lacey takes a little longer with her potty training and doesn't make this problematic connection between edible treats and her sense of self-worth.

Chapter 11

HOW WE TALK ABOUT FOOD

Language matters. The words we use – especially the words we use in the presence of children – describe and even create the world we inhabit. Many ways of talking about food are culturally normal and we are not in the habit of questioning (or noticing) them. For example, we might say we 'deserve' a cake or 'can't have' a biscuit. We might describe food as 'good' or 'naughty'. Children pick up on these subtle cues as they develop their own relationship with food.

In this chapter, we'll be looking at how what we say about food can influence children. We'll consider the moral messages we accidently convey; messages caught up with body image and messages that split food into 'good food' and 'bad food'. We'll also think about messages involving our own food preferences. Throughout the chapter, we'll explore psychologically healthy ways of talking about food in front of children. This chapter does not explore how to talk to children about food in relation to teaching about nutrition. That will be covered in Section 6.

MORAL MESSAGES

Someone offers you a biscuit. Even if you are planning to take one, you might still say 'I shouldn't'. Let's examine this response. By saying 'I shouldn't' you are implying that it is wrong to take the biscuit. By taking it anyway, you imply that it is so tempting, you can't resist.

Thinking back to the concept of self-regulation, we know that a positive relationship with food is one where a child (or adult) eats in response to their body's signals. If an adult uses language that implies guilt ('naughty but nice') or demonstrates eating decisions which contradict their initial intentions ('oh…go on then!') they are not demonstrating self-regulation. More than that, they are modelling guilt in relation to eating and framing that food as something both bad and desirable. The biscuit becomes laden with moral and emotional meaning.

If you are offered a biscuit and say 'yes please', all a watching child will learn is that you wanted a biscuit. If you say 'no thank you', they will learn that you didn't want a biscuit. Either of these is fine – whether or not you accept the biscuit is immaterial. But as soon as words like 'shouldn't' or 'naughty' are used, children will begin to absorb a sense that sweet, calorific foods have a specific status and are mixed up with complex feelings about the self.

BODY IMAGE

These days, body image is a hot topic and recent research from the Professional Association of Childcare and Early Years (PACEY) found that children as young as three are not happy with their bodies. Nearly a quarter of early years practitioners surveyed had seen signs of body dissatisfaction in three- to five-year-olds in their care.[1]

Body image is complex. Children's views of what constitutes an ideal body (as well as their beliefs and feelings about their own bodies) will be heavily influenced by home and wider societal factors. But like so many other aspects of caring for children, just because early years education is not the whole picture, that doesn't mean that it can't be a significant force for good. Helping children develop a positive body image deserves an entire book in its own right. However, there are a few ways to avoid some common linguistic pitfalls.

First, diets. A recent survey of British adults found that almost half of all British adults are trying to lose weight at any one time.[2] The chances of this statistic being replicated in the early years workforce is high. It is also worth noting that most early years practitioners are female and the likelihood of women being on a diet is statistically greater than for men. This has implications for children, because the language and behaviour of the adults around them is hugely influential.

If you are on a diet, you are much more likely to use unhelpful language around food. This is because a diet sets out a blueprint for how we intend to eat. This can clash with what we actually want to eat, leading to moral and emotional statements about food. Here are some suggestions regarding good practice for any early years practitioners on a diet:

- Never talk about being on a diet in front of children.

- Never talk about wanting to lose weight in front of children.

- Never speak negatively about your body in front of children.

- Avoid moral words like 'shouldn't' or 'naughty' in relation to food.

Sometimes, as adults, we talk affectionately about children's bodies in relation to food. If a child eats a lot, we might ask them if their legs are hollow or call them a 'piggy'. If they don't eat much, we might call them 'Skinny Minnie' or tell them they will 'waste away'. Commenting on children's eating like this is very unhelpful. This is especially true when there is also an implicit message about their physical appearance. Sadly, as they grow up, children will be bombarded with messages about how they look. Let's protect them from this as far as we possibly can in early years.

Labelling can also take place in relation to picky eating. Describing a child in their hearing as 'picky', 'fussy' or similar is not at all constructive. Children live up to the expectations we impose upon them and labelling them like this simply adds to their sense of their own limitations.

GOOD FOOD AND BAD FOOD

In this culture, we seem to have reached a place where food perceived as unhealthy has been categorised as 'bad' and food perceived as healthy is labelled 'good'. A better, more subtle notion is one of balance. Kale would become 'bad' if it was all we ate for ten days! Language plays a big part in this dichotomy.

When we describe some food as hard work and some as a treat ('eat your cabbage then you can have some ice cream') we are talking about the cabbage as though it has a different status from the ice cream. The ideal is to level the playing field...to use the same language for all kind of foods and get as excited and enthusiastic about the raw carrot at snack time as the chocolate sponge pudding for lunch.

It's fine to be passionate and excited about food, but we need to be mindful about what we are communicating. Are we putting treat foods up on a pedestal? Are we conveying a moral or emotional message? Avoiding these things is hard because it is not what we are used to as a society, but it is an important part of helping children develop a positive relationship with food.

FOOD PREFERENCES

We all have things we like and dislike. Having been forced to eat my sweetcorn after a two-hour stand-off at junior school, I haven't been able to stomach it since. How we talk about these preferences matters. Children look up to the adults who look after them and if Miss Brown says she hates mushrooms, what are the chances that half the children in the room will say that they do too?

I'm not suggesting that adults' likes and dislikes become closely guarded secrets, never to be spoken of again. In fact, modelling trying a food that you dislike can be very powerful. The challenge is to express dislikes in a constructive way. Miss Brown could have said that she wasn't sure about mushrooms, but she was going to try a small bite to see whether today would be the day that she will like them.

Saying we can't stand a certain kind of food is a very clear cut example of conveying a negative message. However, sometimes what we communicate can be very subtle. An early years practitioner recently told me about a colleague who brought in the children's lunch at the nursery where she worked, saying, 'Who's going to be brave and try the tofu?' She had inadvertently set the tofu up as hard work and potentially not very nice, before it had even got to the children's plates.

I recommend using constructive language in relation to food. When I work therapeutically with very limited eaters, we talk about *foods we really like*, *foods we're learning to like* and *foods we haven't learned to like yet*. This way of talking about food is very powerful for all children, not just picky eaters. It keeps the door open rather than slamming it shut! Children quickly learn to use this terminology and very naturally adopt the mindset-shift that goes with it. Let's focus on possibility, positivity and aspirations rather than what we 'can't' or 'don't' do. In Chapter 19, I share US sociologist and feeding specialist, Dr Dina Rose's take on how we talk about dislikes.

● Chapter 12 ───────────────────────────────

REFLECTING ON YOUR OWN RELATIONSHIP WITH FOOD

In the last chapter, we considered the importance of choosing your words carefully when it comes to talking about food in front of children. Some of the factors which affect how we talk about food could be described as cultural norms. We see the world in a certain way because everyone around us sees and describes it like that. However, another important factor to be aware of when thinking about how you talk about eating is your own relationship with food. This affects both how you respond to children's eating and how you talk about food in front of them.

In this chapter, you will have the opportunity to consider how you relate to food. Until you have been able to process this, it is very hard to truly examine how you work with children's eating. This comes with a bit of a health warning: for some people, their relationship with food is uncomplicated and positive. For others, it can be extremely emotive and complex. Please look after yourself – if you find thinking about some of the ideas covered in this chapter at all distressing, speak to your line manager, a close friend or even a professional counsellor.

YOUR UPBRINGING

Like all aspects of our psyche, our relationship with food is heavily influenced by childhood experiences. How you were brought up in relation to food is likely to have had a significant impact on how you think and feel about food, as well as your eating behaviours.

If you grew up in a household where money was very tight, food may have been a scarce resource. That could make it hard for you to tolerate waste, and could also instil an unconscious response to food whereby you have an instinct to eat as much as possible when food is available.

Think back to Chapter 10 about food being used to reward or punish. Maybe you were punished by having meals withheld as a child. Maybe you were rewarded for good behaviour with sweet treats. Perhaps you had a significant family member who expressed love and approval by giving you certain foods. If you associate food with any of these situations, it can be hard not to automatically replicate these behaviours.

Another response to childhood experiences is to reject aspects of your upbringing. For example, maybe you were made to finish the food that was on your plate or were forced to go to bed without anything to eat if you had misbehaved. Perhaps you have decided never to put another child through that; the pendulum can swing too far the other way and you can find yourself having an excessively permissive attitude to food. This could give you the urge to give children snacks throughout the day or to give them a lot of extra attention when they say they dislike something.

YOUR BODY IMAGE

We touched on body image and dieting in the last chapter. If you have a difficult relationship with your body, first, know that you are not alone. According to a 2015 YouGov survey,[1] more than a third of British adults say they are not happy with their body. Since body dissatisfaction is so commonplace, many people have never really stood back and questioned what it may mean for them.

If you think your relationship with your body may be tied up with your thoughts and feelings about your eating, try to process this. By thinking all of these things through in an honest and reflective way, you will gain awareness. This increased level of insight will enable you to become more conscious about how you manage food in relation to the children in your care.

YOUR BELIEFS

Our beliefs come from all sorts of places, for example: what we read; our cultural, ethnic and religious backgrounds; how we were parented; as well as our life experiences. Here are some examples of food beliefs. Think about how these could have an impact on how you manage food in a professional context:

Food waste is very wrong.

Children should eat everything on their plates.

Children should not be allowed pudding if they don't eat their main course.

Well behaved children should be allowed sweets.

It is the adult's job to 'get food down a child'.

If I 'get a child to eat', I have been nurturing.

PROCESSING COMPLEX THOUGHTS AND FEELINGS ABOUT FOOD

In order to get to grips with your relationship with food, and what this might mean for your professional practice, see if you can summarise all of your food beliefs. It might be helpful to do this with a trusted friend or colleague, or as a team exercise. See if you can establish where each belief comes from. Next, consider your culture and upbringing in relation to food. Do you have the same approach to food and eating as your parents did? If it is different, can you pinpoint how and why this is?

Be mindful that food can be a very sensitive area for some people. If you decide to look at food beliefs as a team, it is essential that you ensure everyone is happy to take part and that appropriate support is available to anyone who finds it hard. Of course, staff members should only share what they are comfortable sharing.

For some people, eating issues can be very complex and challenging indeed. If this is true for you, it's important to seek professional support when it comes to processing your feelings. A qualified counsellor will be able to support you as you explore your relationship with food. If this is something you feel you need to do and are ready to do, it will not only have a positive impact on you at a personal level, it will also be beneficial to your professional practice.

SACHA'S STORY

Sacha is a teacher in a large UK primary school. She runs the Foundation Stage. Sacha was brought up in a family where food was scarce. Her mother had substance misuse issues and Sacha is sure that had she been on the radar of social services, she would have been classified as a child who was at risk of neglect. Sacha often went hungry when she was small and she feels that this has had a lasting effect on her attitudes to food.

At snack time, the children are given milk and a piece of fruit. Some of the children in Sacha's class don't like fruit at all. Others have very limited preferences and will only eat one or two kinds of fruit. The school's policy is to give every child a piece of fruit even if they say they won't eat it. Sometimes a child will take a small bite and then decide to leave it. Sacha finds this incredibly distressing; it makes her very angry and she does everything she possibly can to get the children in her class to eat more of their fruit. She always remains professional, but the situation is emotionally loaded for her and she ends up using some of the controlling feeding practices described in Section 2.

One day, Sacha is very frustrated when she sees the bin overflowing with uneaten fruit. During her break, she sits down in the staff room and cries. The head teacher sees her distress and chats to Sacha about what is wrong, ultimately suggesting she accesses some counselling so she can better understand her strong emotional reaction to food waste. Sacha accepts this suggestion and after several counselling sessions, she has a clearer grasp of the multiple ways in which her relationship with food has been affected by her difficult childhood. She still finds it hard when children leave food but, because she has more insight into why this is, somehow her reactions are less intense and more manageable.

Sacha's case is extreme, but there is a lesson there for all of us. Even if what you have taken from your childhood is positive, you will still have a whole raft of beliefs and feelings about food which you can trace back to how you were brought up. The key is knowing what these are and having thought about how these might affect your behaviours in a professional context. With this knowledge and self-awareness, you can make sure that your practice is always as considered and conscious as possible.

MODELLING

An important consequence of our own relationships with food is what and how we ourselves eat. In Chapter 19, we will be looking at the concept of modelling. This is all about how your eating behaviours can influence the children you work with. The ideas we have looked at in the current chapter are relevant here, because our eating behaviours are of course, underpinned by our relationship with food. If a lot has come up for you during this chapter, you might want to read Chapter 19 now, in order to crystallise your thinking about any implications for practice.

IMPLICATIONS FOR PRACTICE

Fostering a positive relationship with food

In this section, we will look at some of the more practical aspects of helping children develop a positive relationship with food. We will explore best practice in relation to the structure and content of meals, along with an examination of your statutory obligations concerning nutrition. I will introduce 'family-style serving', an American approach which is supportive of psychologically healthy eating. Finally, we will look at staff training because this is a cornerstone of embedding good practice across the whole setting.

——————————————————

Chapter 13

STRUCTURE

Maintaining a consistent and appropriate schedule for meals and snacks is an essential part of helping children develop a positive relationship with food. Here is a summary of the main advantages of a strong structure:

- It enhances children's ability to self-regulate.

- Children feel secure when their day contains elements of routine.

- Children who are anxious eaters benefit from being able to predict when food will be available.

- A strong structure helps ensure that children have an appetite at mealtimes.

WHAT SHOULD THE STRUCTURE LOOK LIKE?

There is no 'set in stone' answer to this question. Experts agree that young children need regular snacks alongside three meals a day. The Infant and Toddler Forum (an organisation providing excellent evidence-based information about feeding young children – see the Resources section) recommends two or three snacks a day for toddlers.[1] Four- and five-year-olds may need fewer snacks, perhaps one or two a day alongside three main meals.

The important thing is to establish a structure and then keep to it. If your setting offers breakfast, you may have breakfast available between 7.30 and 8.00 a.m. This could be followed by a mid-morning snack (often fruit and milk) at 10.00 a.m. Then lunch might be served at midday. Leaving lunch too late can result in children eating less well because they are getting tired, especially those who have an afternoon sleep. Then an afternoon snack could be offered at 2.30 p.m.

Getting the structure right involves striking a balance, avoiding leaning towards either giving children food too frequently or not frequently enough. In order to help children eat in response to their appetite, I recommend leaving at least two hours between each eating opportunity. As young children's stomachs are small, you must also be mindful of not leaving too much time between meals and snacks. Three hours is the longest gap you should leave.[2]

ROLLING SNACKS

It has recently become fashionable in early years to offer what are sometimes termed 'rolling snacks'. This is where children are given access to snacks over a long period of time. They can help themselves when they feel they want something. I believe that this way of providing snacks is extremely unhelpful. Children miss out on the social and emotional lessons learned during a communal eating opportunity. They miss out on learning from their peers' (and staff's) example. It is also harder to maintain good hygiene and make sure that children have washed their hands before they eat. Importantly, children's appetite may also be negatively affected if they choose to eat too close to a main meal.

I have come across various arguments in favour of rolling snacks, including the idea that it supports independence and gives children choice. By making more than one thing available at snack time, children can be given a limited choice. By serving themselves, they can develop independence. Too great a choice can be overwhelming for children. There are many ways to encourage autonomy in an early years environment and I would argue that the disadvantages of rolling snacks far outweigh any benefits.

MILK

In the UK, milk is currently provided free for all children under five in a registered setting. This is great from a nutritional perspective, as milk is an important part of young children's diets. Children who are registered to have milk should be offered it along with their morning or afternoon snack. Serving it separately will have a negative impact on their appetites and should be seen as an eating opportunity in itself. For example, if children have fruit at 10.00 then milk at 11.00 and lunch at midday, they will not be very hungry when they sit down for lunch. If they have their milk with their fruit at 10.00, they are likely to eat better at their midday meal.

AVOIDING BAD PRACTICE

The following scenarios include some common pitfalls where the meal and snack structure is not conducive to children eating well.

Having eating opportunities too close together

Sometimes, the morning snack is offered at 10.30 and then lunch is served an hour or so later. Children will have insufficient appetite and may then eat less of their lunch, which is usually more nutritionally dense.

Having too many eating opportunities (grazing)

If children have lots of snacks as well as main meals, they will miss out on the experience of the natural daily rhythm of fullness and hunger. This rhythm is such an important aspect of self-regulation. If children graze, their physiological eating cues (appetite) will be masked and they will be less able to tune in to what their bodies need. As described above, milk should also be taken into consideration when thinking about this. However, children should have unlimited access to water all day long.

Inadvertently giving children an incentive not to eat

An early years practitioner recently told me that she had changed the way she offered children their fruit. She used to give it to them just before their playtime, but noticed that children were throwing it in the bin because they wanted to hurry off and play with their friends. Now she gives them their fruit after playtime and far more gets eaten! Try to see things from a child's perspective and make sure you're not giving them a reason to hurry or reject their food.

Being inconsistent

Occasionally, settings offer afternoon snacks on some days but not others. This is very problematic psychologically, because children don't know what to expect. It is unhelpful physically, because the ideal is for children to get used to a regular pattern of eating in order to support self-regulation. Best practice is thinking carefully about your schedule and then sticking to it.

Reviewing your schedule

Although consistency is essential, sometimes you might find you need to tweak your schedule. Maybe you've noticed that many children are not eating much at lunchtime. Look at making your morning snack slightly earlier. Perhaps children seem fragile and low in energy during the afternoon. Consider offering an afternoon snack or, if you are already offering one, move it forward. You could also look carefully at the nutritional content of what you are offering to make sure it is meeting children's needs.

When you are thinking of changing your schedule (or are implementing a new schedule for the first time) try it out for a couple of weeks before deciding if it is working for the children in your setting. Children take a little while to get used to a new structure. Once finalised, include your meal and snack schedule in your food policy (see Chapter 22) so that parents know when their children will be eating.

Chapter 14

CONTENT

In the last chapter, we considered *when* to offer children food. This chapter looks at *what* to offer. This book does not provide detailed information about nutrition. If you want to know more about children's nutritional needs, you will find some suggested further reading in the Resources section. We will be looking at your statutory obligations though, as well as thinking about practicalities like menu planning.

RING THE CHANGES

Earlier in the book when we considered some key concepts in relation to feeding children, we looked closely at variety and exposure. It is impossible to overstate just how important it is to provide a varied diet, both from the point of view of health and of giving the children in your care a positive relationship with food. Variety is one of the basic principles of healthy eating, as eating a wider range of different foods provides a better balance of nutrients.

Offering a varied diet is very difficult without good menu planning. When you plan what food will be provided in your setting, try to push the boundaries a little and forget about what our culture has decided is 'kids' food'. There is nothing to saying that children need to eat a bland, repetitive diet except that this is what they and their families may have been socially conditioned to accept and expect. Of course, children's health and safety should always be your priority and you must consider things like salt content and choking hazards.

Health precautions aside, there is no reason why you can't introduce children to a wide variety of foods, including dishes from other cultures and things they may never have come across before. You might like to build novelty into your menu in a formulaic way when you come to menu plan. For example, you could make sure that every week you serve a food that has not been served before in your setting.

It is also a very good idea to maintain a high level of variety from within the context of the same dishes. For example, if you serve cottage pie, one week include swede in the mash. Another week, include sweet potato. Another time, you could add some chopped parsley. This is because if children become used to things being slightly different, they will develop confidence when it comes to trying new foods. When children are served a limited number of meals on rotation, unfamiliar foods can become really threatening.

Planning small changes to old favourites is another great way of introducing novelty in a manageable way. From a child's perspective, it is much less intimidating to try sweet potato for the first time when it is mixed with mashed potato as part of their favourite cottage pie, than it is to have sweet potato served by itself. There is even scope for maintaining novelty in the context of staples like bread or pasta. Try multi-coloured pasta or different pasta shapes. Use different types of bread, including bread products from other cuisines, like wholemeal pitta.

Providing a varied diet takes extra time and effort. When you are catering on a large scale, of course buying in bulk and repeat ordering makes economic sense. However, working within the resources at your disposal, the more varied the food you provide, the better this will be for the children attending your setting.

BE RELENTLESS!

In Chapter 4, we explored the research into how many exposures to a new food may be required before a child learns to accept it. We also looked at the mismatch between this and how often new foods are actually offered. Some children take to unfamiliar foods very quickly, but for others it can take multiple exposures before they learn to accept something a little bit different.

Relentlessly offer new foods again and again until they become familiar. It can be interesting to do an experiment with this. Pick one food that you have not served before, for example courgette. Then serve it on 20 separate occasions. Make a note of how many children accept it each time and see whether you can observe the impact of the increased levels of familiarity with each exposure. It is a good idea to leave at least a few days between each instance you offer it.

INCLUDE 'EASY' FOODS

A big part of making new foods manageable is to make sure that as well as something new and different, you also serve something that most children reliably accept. For children who are not confident eaters, it makes a big difference to them if they know from experience that there will always be something available that they are comfortable eating. For example, when you try courgette, you might also have carrots – a common vegetable that many children enjoy because it is sweet tasting and familiar.

USE OPTIMUM TIMES TO INTRODUCE NOVELTY

For children who are cautious (or downright terrified) about eating new foods, it can make a big difference *when* you introduce them. Take time to notice when the majority of children seem to have the most positive eating experience. Do they eat best at breakfast, if this is provided? Snack time is best for many children. If you are employed by a nursery or are a childminder providing an evening meal, you may have noticed that children often struggle with their evening meal, as they are tired and potentially over-stimulated after a long day.

It is a good idea to pay attention to these nuances and offer the most challenge in terms of novelty, at children's optimum times. There's no reason why breakfast has to be just toast or cereal, or why snack time has to be an apple, orange or banana. Offering variety is all about being creative and thinking outside the box, while adhering to nutritional guidelines.

KNOW YOUR OBLIGATIONS

Early years settings need to be familiar with their statutory obligations in relation to the nutritional content of meals. The Statutory Framework for the Early Years Foundation Stage (hereafter referred to as the EYFS Framework) includes a welfare requirement for the provision of food and drink, which states, 'Where children are provided with meals, snacks and drinks, they must be healthy, balanced and nutritious' and 'fresh drinking water must be available and accessible at all times'.[1] Voluntary guidance[2] has been produced by the Children's Food Trust which translates what this means in practice, by providing evidence-based, age-appropriate advice on why and how to provide healthy, balanced and nutritious food for young children.

The food and drink guidelines emphasise dietary diversity by encouraging settings to provide a variety of foods from the four main food groups (starchy foods, fruit and vegetables, meat and alternatives and dairy foods). Additional guidance on limiting saturated fat, salt and added sugar and guidelines for drinks and cakes and desserts is also included. The guidelines also include typical portion sizes for a range of foods, but emphasise that the appetites of young children will vary, and they should be encouraged to eat healthy food according to their appetite.

The food-based guidelines are built on a nutritional framework, enabling settings to provide nutritious and balanced food without having to do nutrient calculations themselves.[3] A series of practical tools, including a menu planning checklist and an 'Early Years Code of Practice for Food and Drink' have also been developed by the Trust, to support early years settings to effectively implement the food and drink guidelines, and share their approach to food with parents and other visitors.

In addition to the requirements of the EYFS Framework, maintained nursery schools, and nursery classes within maintained primary schools (the situation with academies and free schools is more complex) are required to meet the mandatory food-based standards for school lunches outlined in Schedule 5 of the 2014 School Food Regulations.[4] These Regulations require that one item from each of four food groups (fruit and vegetables, starchy foods, meat, fish and alternatives and milk and dairy foods) is provided at lunchtime each day.

The revised school food standards came into force on 1 January, 2015. According to Julie Hargadon OBE (former chief executive of the Children's Food Trust) the national standards have transformed how children eat in schools.[5] The relevant documents are available to download from the government website.[6] The standards apply to food served to children as part of a normal day. Celebrations, fundraising events and food served as part of a cultural event are exempt, as is food provided by parents on an occasional basis. Food prepared as part of a cookery class is also not covered by these standards.

MENU PLANNING

Many settings use a rotating menu with perhaps two or three weeks' meals. If it is feasible in terms of cost and staffing, I recommend having as long a rotation period as possible in order to increase variety in the children's diets. Maybe you could design seasonal menus on a three- or four-week rotation, which you could develop and update year on year.

In June 2016, Public Health England commissioned the Children's Food Trust to develop a series of example menus for early years settings in England to support early years practitioners to provide meals and snacks in line with current government dietary recommendations. At the time of writing, these have not yet been published by the government. However, if you visit the Children's Food Trust website (see the Resources section) you will be signposted to the menus as soon as they are available. The Children's Food Trust website is an excellent source of evidence-based, age-appropriate nutrition information for anyone working in early years who has an interest in children's food and nutrition and you will find lots of extremely useful practical resources there.

Good planning is essential, because it will enable you to meet children's nutritional needs by looking at what they have eaten over the course of a week rather than day by day. It also saves money and time.

> Effective planning helps you keep things varied and enables you to ensure that you are regularly offering new and different foods, while meeting children's needs in terms of nutrition.

Think about how you can incorporate repeated exposures into your meal planning. Going back to the example using courgette, if you plan that in as a new food to try, make sure you plan it in again on repeated occasions over the ensuing weeks. You might also like to change the days with each menu rotation, so children who only attend your setting one or two days a week get the maximum exposure to a varied diet.

SEASONAL FOOD

Cooking seasonally links in very well in terms of bringing food into the curriculum and helping children engage with where their food comes from. It is also good practice from an environmental point of view. It helps you maintain a high level of variety, as your menu will change as you go through the year. If you are able to grow food with the children, it is lovely to tie this into your meal planning so they can literally enjoy eating the fruits of their labour!

——————————————

Chapter 15

SERVING FAMILY-STYLE

Many American feeding specialists recommend an approach to feeding children which is referred to in the USA as 'family-style' serving. American feeding expert Maryann Jacobsen describes how family-style meals work:

> Serve items separately in bowls and allow children to serve themselves (with help from parents [adults] as needed). In addition to giving kids the control they crave, family-style meals help those younger than six who have a need for things to be 'just right' and prefer food that doesn't touch.[1]

Family-style meals are great for all children, especially picky eaters. If children are able to serve themselves, this offers innumerable opportunities for them to practise many valuable skills.

You may be wondering how this approach to meals can be successful in an early years setting. It is certainly easier in the context of a childminder's home (or a family home). This is simply because of the levels of supervision required in order to allow children to safely and effectively serve themselves. It is possible to make it work in other early years settings, however, especially with the older children. This is illustrated by the case study in Chapter 39, featuring a setting in New Zealand where family-style serving is working extremely well, alongside other excellent, forward-thinking feeding practices.

Here are some of the general advantages of family-style serving:

- Children build social skills, such as turn taking, waiting for others and thinking about other children's needs.

- Children's communication skills are boosted as they practise asking for things to be passed, and respond to their peers' requests.

- Children practise their motor skills.

- Children feel more involved and engaged with the meal as they have an active role to play.

And these are advantages which are especially supportive of picky eaters:

- Children are exposed to a wide range of foods even if they don't eat them.

- Children's anxiety is minimised through the control they are given over the food on their plate.

- Children are not singled out or made to feel different, because they are not served different meals.

It can be very daunting for a picky eater to be given a plate piled high with foods which they do not want to eat. This can immediately start the meal off on a negative note for that child, potentially generating anxiety which can have a negative impact on appetite. In my experience, a child is much more likely to try a food if they have been given control over the serving of it. As American feeding experts Katja Rowell and Jenny McGlothlin write in their fantastic book for parents of extremely picky eaters:

> If you preplate your child's meals with what and how much you want her to eat, the battle probably begins before the plate hits the table: 'I don't like that!' 'It's touching!' 'How much do I have to eat?' Your child's focus is on the negotiation, and her appetite plummets.[2]

Family-style service promotes the idea that preferences are in flux. Children feel less need to communicate their dislikes and cling to their preferences, because they have the freedom to choose what goes on their plates. We may not like something today, but we might like it tomorrow. Children don't need to make negative statements about their meal – 'but I don't like carrots!' – because they are in control of whether or not they put carrots on their plate.

In the USA, both governmental and non-governmental agencies have been recommending family-style service as best practice in childcare settings since the 1990s.[3] The university of Idaho is a centre of excellence in relation to child feeding in group settings and provides fantastic online resources (see the Resources section). Researchers from the university carried out a study exploring some of the criticisms of family-style service, namely that it increases levels of food waste and makes meals last too long. They found neither to be the case.[4]

Family-style serving has many clear benefits for children and can greatly enhance the sense of community at meal and snack times. However, for me, the most important advantage it confers is how supportive it is of children's ability to self-regulate. Self-regulation is a concept that I return to time and again in this book, because it really is at the heart of a positive relationship with food. Serving family-style enables us to trust children to trust themselves. It may not be the easiest option in an early years setting, but best practice often isn't!

Chapter 16

STAFF TRAINING

If you manage a nursery or are the lead practitioner in a setting, you can have all the good intentions in the world when it comes to how you want to do things but, without the support of your team, it is almost impossible to achieve your vision. Training is a very important part of ensuring that your staff are onside. This is not only about informing your colleagues about best practice, but is also about ensuring that they understand *why* you are asking them to do things in a certain way. If your team understand the principles behind the practices, they are much more likely to fully embrace them.

You can share reading material with your staff team. You will find suggested further reading in the Resources section at the end of the book. You can give them a copy of this book, too, but not everyone has the time or inclination to read. You need to provide hands-on training so that your team has a genuine understanding of what good practice looks like, in relation to food.

THE COOK

Being a school or nursery cook is not easy. There are high expectations about the standard of food that must be produced but, in many cases, time and money to support this are in short supply. The following quotation provides a snapshot of the state of training for school cooks. It is reasonable to assume that a similar picture exists in early years:

> While some caterers and schools offer excellent training, this is not the norm. Many school cooks learn their kitchen skills on the job. The lucky ones may get to turn their hands to all sorts of things,

from buying ingredients and cooking from scratch to butchering their own meat. But in other schools, catering staff may find themselves doing not much more than arranging the food in the serving areas or reheating pre-cooked meals. Formal training for school catering staff is often patchy. The emphasis tends to be on hygiene and safety training, which are required by law, rather than on cooking. The most recent Children's Food Trust annual survey found that the vast majority (90%) of local authorities offered their catering staff training in Food Hygiene, Basic Induction and Food Safety, but only 19% offered the level 2 Kitchen Skills Diploma, which actually teaches cooking.[1]

We need to value our cooks and support their professional development. It is not reasonable to expect cooks to produce good food if there has been insufficient investment in their training.

THE MIDDAY SUPERVISOR

Midday supervisors are often teaching staff with a dual role, or perhaps they come in for a few hours each day to cover lunch time. It is a job that is often overlooked. In fact, the midday supervisor has the potential to have an extremely positive influence over the eating environment. A head teacher once told me that it was very difficult to train her midday supervisors because she was not prepared to pay them for their time beyond their standard working hours, and during the hours they were in school, their time was spoken for.

Schools (and other settings) need to value staff who only come in to supervise mealtimes. They need to invest in their workforce and recognise the importance of this role. It is great for practitioners to have an understanding of good mealtime practice, but often they are not the ones on the front line when children are eating.

This is especially true for early years settings attached to a primary school. Many midday supervisors come in every day and may do playground duty as well as helping with the food. The chances are, they will know the children very well. Empower midday supervisors and develop their professional capacity through training; they are uniquely placed to have a positive influence on children's relationship with food.

FOCUS POINTS

Comprehensive guidance on staff training is beyond the remit of this book, but here a few things to consider.

Induction
Add an 'all about food' section to your staff induction procedure. Make sure new staff understand the way you do things, are happy to commit to supporting your ideals and have an opportunity to ask any questions they may have. Arrange for new staff members to observe a meal or snack time where experienced staff demonstrate pressure-free mealtimes in action.

Your food policy
It is good practice to use and develop a food policy – something we will be looking later on in this book. You can use this as part of your induction and staff can be given a copy of it alongside other key policies and procedures.

Food ambassadors
Every staff member who ever has anything to do with children's eating needs to be trained in best practice. However, it is a good idea to have a few key team members who have particularly in-depth knowledge. Choose one or two colleagues to be 'food ambassadors'. They can show other members of the team what best practice looks like, and could even potentially run training sessions for other team members.

Workshops based on this book
If you are confident about the ideas you have read about in this book, you could consider running workshops for your colleagues, themed around individual chapters.

External training resources
See the Resources section for a selection of relevant training options for early years practitioners. We are all constantly learning and growing; prioritising training is an essential aspect of good practice. In this era of budgetary challenges, sadly funding training is not always easy.

HOW TO SUCCEED

As you will see when you read the case study about up-to-date, evidence-based good practice used in a nursery in New Zealand, it takes time to embed a new approach to food. Here are a few ways to avoid common pitfalls.

Don't give up too soon

As anyone who works with children will know, when confronted with a new way of doing things or a new set of boundaries, children will test whether these changes are permanent. The way they test a boundary or a new system is often to push against it. You may find that when you start using the kinds of approaches detailed in this book, children initially respond negatively.

Remain strong in the face of resistance from colleagues

Just like with the children, expect a little resistance from colleagues. Use empathy to try to understand why they may be feeling unwilling to take on a new way of doing things. Some people (most people!) find change really hard. There is security in 'but we have always done it like this'.

Feeding is extremely emotive. Asking colleagues to stop seeing their role as what I refer to as 'get food down child' is actually asking something pretty big of them. They may be parents themselves – you could be asking them to indirectly reassess how they feed their family. They may have been brought up with very strong food rules. For example, in childhood, they may have been punished for not eating everything on their plate. Just as these values, beliefs and practices form slowly over time, they take time to leave behind, too.

Justify your thinking

By explaining that these ideas have their basis in research and are supported by feeding specialists across the globe, you can help sceptical team members get on board. It is a cultural norm here in the UK to see it as our role to encourage children to eat more – to control their eating. Challenging socially accepted ways of doing things is very difficult. Just remember that because we have done something a certain way since time immemorial, that doesn't mean those practices are right. There are lots of examples from the world of childcare and early years where this is illustrated. For example, we used to force left-handed children to write with their right hand, a practice that would be unthinkable these days.

Be consistent

When people first start moving away from controlling feeding practices (see Section 2) there is often an interim period while these ideas really bed-in, where it can be very hard to be consistent. This is simply because old habits die hard. You may not think you're being controlling at all, when you hear yourself telling a child to 'eat up' or 'try just one more bite'. Perhaps you could set up a system where team members commit to reminding each other when they inadvertently depart from best practice. That way, everyone would be learning together and no one need feel criticised or defensive.

The key to making good practice stick in your setting is to keep on reiterating the message. You must also lead by example and make sure that good practice in relation to food is embedded across your whole setting, and is not just an optional 'add-on'. Ultimately, the whole team will see how beneficial creating a positive eating environment can be. This is not just in terms of children accessing a wider diet, but is also about mealtimes being fun and relaxed. This is better for the children but it is also better for staff.

YOUR FOOD ETHOS

In this section, we will think about what an ideal eating environment entails and how to create it. We will consider the space itself, where you focus your attention as a practitioner, and the importance of what adults model. We will look at the social side of eating: how to make meals about coming together and connecting with one another. These things all contribute to your overall food ethos: a sense of what matters to you, what you believe and how you choose to be in relation to food.

Chapter 17

THE EATING ENVIRONMENT

A low-stimulation, relaxed and positive eating environment is the ideal that we are striving for. Real life sometimes gets in the way; children may be upset or tired, and staff are only human too. But if you can make a concerted effort to make eating a positive experience for everyone, this will become a 'virtuous circle': the nicer the environment, the better the children will eat and the more relaxed everyone will feel.

THE PROBLEM WITH CONFLICT

Research[1] shows that conflict is extremely unhelpful in terms of children's eating. In particular, it makes picky eating worse. Conflict can come in many forms. Perhaps the children are bickering with one another. Perhaps staff are responding with negatively to children's challenging behaviour at the table. Without a commitment to avoiding controlling feeding practices, there could potentially even be conflict or tension about what and how much the children are eating,

Make sure language is kept positive; instead of talking about the behaviour you don't want to see, hone in on the behaviour you want to nurture. In her excellent book about positive behaviour management in early years settings, Liz Williams writes:

> Although it may seem overly simplistic, just by concentrating on using positive language, and by using it frequently, adults can have an impact on children's behaviour. Describe the behaviours you want to see.[2]

Children's table manners can often become a source of negativity. There is a very fine line between helping children develop appropriate mealtime skills and behaviours, and being excessively critical of how they are eating. In Chapter 27, we will be thinking about what exactly manners are, which manners matter and how to teach manners away from the table. In order to maintain a conflict-free environment, make sure any intervention is gentle and calm, and focus on supporting lots of positive social interaction during meals.

> If you are no longer concerned with what and how much the children are eating, this gives you space to focus on helping them enjoy one another's company.

SENSORY STIMULATION

Sensory sensitivity has been linked to picky eating in children,[3] although some research points to certain types of sense data being more significant than others.[4] I find that children who struggle with sensory processing often benefit from a low level of sensory stimulation during mealtimes. You can learn more about how sensory processing affects eating in Chapter 36.

Let's think about the sense data generated by a plate of food: we see it, we smell it…ultimately, we taste it. We have a tactile experience of its texture, temperature and shape. This can be hard work for a little brain! Often, communal dining rooms are very tricky for children with sensory sensitivity because they are full of sights, sounds and strong smells. In order to help these children cope with the sense data their brains will receive when they are confronted by their food, it can be very helpful to minimise the level of stimulation in the eating environment.

Calm music can work well. Plain walls in the eating area are good too, or displays which are relatively muted and not too busy or colourful. If it is possible to have children eating far from the kitchen, the levels of cooking smells can be reduced. Of course, this needs to be balanced with practical considerations like carrying the food from the kitchen to the eating area, but changes as small as simply keeping the kitchen door shut can make a difference.

Children exhibit differing degrees of sensory sensitivity, but there is one group of children who are particularly likely to be sensory sensitive, and that is autistic children. We will be looking at autism in relation to eating in more depth in Chapter 35 but, for now, it is worth bearing in mind that anything you can do to make your eating environment as relaxed and low-stimulation as possible will be especially beneficial for this vulnerable group. Research[5] also points to children with attention deficit hyperactivity disorder (ADHD) having trouble with sensory processing, beyond the core symptoms of ADHD. Fostering a calm, low-stimulation eating environment will enable you to better support some of those children in your care who have special educational needs or a disability (SEND).

DON'T RUSH IT!

You probably have a lot to cram into your day and may have more than one sitting for meals. Time pressure is a very real constraint, but it is vital to ensure that meals and snacks don't feel rushed. If you are feeling stressed and keen to get children in and out, the children in your care will pick this up and their stress levels may also rise. This is not conducive to their eating well. Researchers have suggested that in young children, increased stress levels reduce appetite because of the associated reduction in gut activity.[6]

Try as hard as you can to make meals relaxed and stress-free. Maybe this could mean making some small changes to your plans for the day, so that you don't feel so much time pressure. If you can eat with the children, this will make it easier to create a relaxed atmosphere. You can stop and enjoy your food with them.

It is a good idea to have a set amount of time for snacks and meals, and to have a visual indicator of timings which children can see or hear. Maybe you could use a sand timer. I suggest allowing approximately 15 minutes for snacks and 30 minutes for main meals. Choose a timing that feels right for your setting and include it in your food policy (see Chapter 22). Be ready to review your timings if you feel meals or snacks are either rushed or dragged out.

The benefits of clear timings are that children become aware (if they are mature enough) of how long they have to eat their food. This means that you don't have to hurry them along; they will simply understand that if they choose not to eat within the allotted timeframe, the food will be taken away because the meal is over. For most children, if they have left a lot of food despite being at the table for half an hour, the chances are, they don't want it. Pressuring children to hurry up can quickly become a controlling feeding practice (see Section 2) and brings stress and negativity into the eating environment.

MAKE IT SPECIAL

There are many ways to make meal and snack times special for children. The more you can communicate that meals are a positive, social experience, the more children will develop positive associations with eating. Here are some ideas of ways you can help make communal eating special:

- Give children special jobs to do.

- Help the children make their own individual placemats.

- Make the table visually attractive with a nice wipeable table cloth, for example.

- Encourage the children to make place names for one another.

- Have special music to go with pre-meal routines such as hand-washing.

If your staff numbers allow, try to have children seated at small tables with maybe six to eight children and an adult. Your ratios will obviously depend on the age of the children in your care. Small tables are generally calmer and an adult can easily maintain a positive atmosphere if they can be heard by all the children at their table. With small tables, there is no need for voices to be raised and it is easy for the adult to notice if an individual child is struggling. Small tables replicate a family environment and are an ideal context for teaching and demonstrating social skills.

When you decide where the children are going to sit, it is a good idea to mix up children with different levels of eating skills so that children who lack skills or are picky eaters can benefit from the positive influence of their peers. Remember never to articulate this, as comparing children to one another is not only shaming, it is also a form of controlling feeding practice. Rather than 'Look, Yasmin is using her fork properly, try and use yours like she does', praise Yasmin for her lovely fork use, and other children will take note. This is an example of separating eating and mealtime behaviour. It is appropriate to praise a child for their behaviour (like Yasmin and her fork) but not for their eating decisions.

If you can develop an ethos where meal and snack times are respected and looked forward to, children will learn that eating communally is a positive experience. Conversely, if they are used to feeling criticised, pressured or rushed during meals, many of the associations they form will be negative.

———————————————————

Chapter 18

THE SOCIAL SIDE OF EATING

So far in this book, we have looked in a lot of detail at what not to do at mealtimes – not to see your role as 'get food down child' and not to exert even the gentlest pressure during meals. So many people (both parents and professionals alike) are very much used to dedicating much of their effort during meals towards getting children to eat. When we take that away, we are left with a bit of a vacuum. And this is the subject of this chapter: what remains when we have lost our old mealtime agenda?

In her book about child development, Catherine Lee talks about what meals are. She writes: 'Meals are more than eating: they are social occasions, an important part of the civilisation in which the child is developing'.[1] I love this quote because it sums up just how significant a role food plays in our lives. What we eat is tied up with our cultural identity, our personalities and our values. At their best, meals are about togetherness and community. When you stop worrying about what children are eating, you can concentrate on fostering the social side of eating.

WHAT DO WE MEAN BY 'SOCIAL'?

The social side of meals includes everything that involves any element of human interaction. Sometimes this is tied into the meal itself, such as asking another person to pass the water. Sometimes it is more about conversation, encompassing listening skills, turn taking and empathy.

Each time children eat communally they are practising valuable social skills. This is especially powerful when they have an adult sitting with them who is able to nurture this skill development.

Personal, social and emotional development is one of the prime areas in the EYFS Framework (2017),[2] specifically, the requirement to help children 'to form positive relationships and develop respect for others; to develop social skills and learn how to manage their feelings [and] to understand appropriate behaviour in groups'.[3] Let's take the three aspects of personal, social and emotional development set out in the framework and look at how each of these can be supported during mealtimes.

SELF-CONFIDENCE AND SELF-AWARENESS

Children have many opportunities to develop their self-confidence and self-awareness while they eat. For example, they can practise asking for help when they need it. Practitioners will be used to achieving a balance between appropriate help (like cutting up some meat that a child is struggling with) and supporting independence (like encouraging a child to have a go at cutting up their meat themselves, in an age-appropriate way).

Trying new or disliked foods requires a certain level of confidence. Equally, when a child goes beyond their comfort zone and tries something new (willingly, of course), this will boost their confidence and self-esteem. By following the guidelines set out in this book, you will be creating an environment and feeding ethos that facilitates experimentation with new foods. By giving children control of their eating decisions (from within the context you set) you are empowering them and building their autonomy.

Meals are a great opportunity to teach children about sharing their ideas and experiences. When the talk is no longer about the food and who is eating what, it can be about everyone's day; about what you will be doing later and all the other wonderful things that populate small children's imaginations. The framework refers to 'confidence to speak in a small group' – communal eating at small tables provides a brilliant opportunity for this.

MANAGING FEELINGS AND BEHAVIOUR

Learning to wait to be served – or to help themselves when it is their turn – is a great opportunity to practise recognising and controlling impulses, like the urge to take some food and eat. It teaches children to be patient and to think of the needs of others. Maybe there are only a few pieces of apple left at snack time and all the children want some. Use this as a chance to work on sharing (and numeracy!).

Understanding and following rules is an important aspect of social and emotional development and has gained in prominence since the recent focus on British Values in UK education. Teaching children why rules matter, and how they link to respecting one another, is essential. Mealtime rules need not be oppressive and complicated; children quickly learn what is expected in relation to their behaviour.

Each meal and snack is a chance for children to practise thinking about and following rules, even ones as simple as washing hands before eating. Meal and snack times help children learn that certain behaviours are unacceptable. By having clear expectations around how children behave at mealtimes, and approaching these consistently, you are developing children's ability to reflect on and manage their behaviour as well as their feelings.

MAKING RELATIONSHIPS

Conversation underpins relationships. Helping children learn to listen to one another and cooperate is a big part of the social side of eating. For example, empathy can be developed by teaching children to reflect back what another child has said. We can build listening skills by gently reminding children to give one another space to say what they want to say. Sometimes this can be done in quite a formulaic way. For example, you could go around the table, each sharing something you enjoyed about the morning, then practise asking the speaker a question about what exactly they enjoyed about that activity. Alternatively, you could let the children take the lead, supporting the conversation as it flows.

Let's look briefly at what researchers have found in relation to language acquisition in young children at mealtimes. A small-scale American study pointed to staff not talking much at all to children during meals, and most interaction being in the form of instructions like 'eat your food'. On the other hand, research looking at Scandinavian practitioners found that they used mealtimes as an opportunity to engage toddlers in a variety of conversational topics.[4] It is easy to see how controlling feeding practices limit the scope for supporting positive interactions. As a practitioner, you can capitalise upon mealtimes to make use of all that potential for developing children's language and relationship-building skills.

Thinking of others is an important learning opportunity to take advantage of at mealtimes. We might express gratitude to the farmer and the cook when we reflect on our food before eating. We might think of others who are not as fortunate as we are and don't have enough to eat. When children are ready to take food (if you use the self-service model I describe in Chapter 15) they can practise checking that others have enough and that no one is left out.

THE ROLE OF THE PRACTITIONER

You have many jobs during meals and snacks:

- making sure children are able to access the food they need
- nurturing conversation
- building social skills
- helping children think of one another
- keeping the atmosphere relaxed and positive.

You don't need to make the children eat their food – that is their job.

TREASURE MEAL AND SNACK TIME

Children eat several times a day and we need to see each of these occasions as a precious opportunity to boost children's personal, social and emotional development. For many children, the meals and snacks they have in your setting could be the only communal eating opportunities in their lives. The value this has for children's wellbeing and growth is impossible to overstate.

MODELLING

If you are an early years practitioner, you will already understand the importance of leading by example. 'Do as I say, not as I do' just doesn't cut it with the under-fives. If you don't want shouting from the children, you don't shout yourself. If you want children to learn how to respect and listen to another, you demonstrate this every single day, in the way you interact with them. Of course, modelling is not just about how you behave towards children, but how you behave towards colleagues, too.[1] Modelling positive behaviour is second nature for competent practitioners, but it is not so widely understood just what an enormous impact adult modelling has on eating behaviours. The following are some of the food-related behaviours that adults might model.

SELF-REGULATION

We want children to learn to eat in response to their internal cues (their appetite) and we want them to stop eating when they experience satiety (fullness). An adult modelling eating in response to appetite might say before a meal, 'My tummy is rumbling! It will be snack time soon and I'm ready for my fruit!' At lunch time, they might be offered second helpings by another staff member, and reply, 'No thank you, I can tell my tummy hasn't got any more room because I haven't got any hungry feelings any more.'

TRYING SOMETHING DIFFERENT

Encouraging children to try foods is not about telling them to have a taste. It's about modelling, exposure and acclimatising them to variety. Imagine you have something a little different at snack time one day, for example, a yellow tomato. An adult might say, 'Oooh – that doesn't look like a normal tomato! Normal tomatoes are red but this one is yellow. I'm interested in how it tastes but I'm not sure about it because it's different. I'll just try a small bite. Wow, it's delicious…and it tastes just like a red tomato.'

Please note, this is very different from a 'hard sell' approach to encouraging children to eat, which I call 'food PR' (a kind of controlling feeding practice), such as extolling the virtues of tomatoes as a way of persuading a child to try some. What you are doing in this example with the yellow tomato is modelling trying a food that is different and that you are a little nervous about. You are modelling it being acceptable to feel a bit unsure about something new, and then trying it anyway.

You can also model trying something new and not liking it, saying, 'I am not sure about how this tastes. Maybe I will like it next time I try it.' This shows children that disliking something is not catastrophic and it is normal. It also teaches them that it is not final. Just because you didn't like something that day, we don't need to leap to an absolute statement of 'I don't like yellow tomatoes.' American child feeding specialist, Dina Rose, suggests talking about trying foods in the context of how many times we need to try something before we might like it. She writes:

> 'John just hasn't tasted the rice enough times yet,' is a great way to frame one person's food preferences for young children. 'I didn't like rice when I was young [states Rose]. Now I love it. That's why it's important to keep tasting.'[2]

TRYING SOMETHING DISLIKED

You can model trying something you previously disliked and maybe even finding that you do like it! Be authentic – there is huge value in taking a genuine risk yourself and trying something that you really aren't sure about. It's only fair to do this yourself, if you hope for the children in your care to have this attitude. And even if it turns out you still don't like it, that's fine. We all have our likes and dislikes and we are all different. The key is to communicate (through your behaviour and language) that these dislikes may not be set in stone and that it's safe to take a small risk and try something new or disliked, whatever the outcome. Make sure dislike is expressed with subtlety because a dramatic rejection will put the children off!

SOCIAL SKILLS

You can model all the social skills we talked about in Chapter 18. Mealtimes are such a rich opportunity to teach turn taking, sharing, thinking of others and communication skills. You can lead the way in terms of guiding the conversation and then model how we listen respectfully when others are talking. When it comes to second helpings, you can express concern about whether others have had enough before taking seconds. You can pass children food items and show them how we ask for something to be passed, by asking yourself.

EATING A VARIED DIET

It sounds obvious, but you can do so much by simply sitting down and tucking into a variety of healthy food. Children look to adults to see what is safe. By sitting down, eating a mushroom and talking about the weather, you are showing children that eating mushrooms is a normal, safe thing to do.

FUN RITUALS

It is a lovely idea to build regular food rituals or occasions into your routine. For example, an early years practitioner working in a primary school in Cornwall told me about how they have 'Fruity Fridays'. Every Friday, the children are asked to bring in a piece of fruit that is unusual – not the bananas, tomatoes, apples or oranges that are supplied at school every day. The fruits are cut up into small pieces and shared with the class. The children love the social experience of sharing the fruits they bring, with the teacher and the other children. They are also getting used to trying things that are a little different.

COMMUNAL EATING

You might have noticed that there is a common thread running through all of these different ways you can model positive eating behaviours. They all involve adults eating with the children! In many settings, this is not the norm. There are lots of reasons for this, not least that when you are still pursuing an agenda of 'get food down child', all that focus on their eating will hardly leave you with the time and energy to stop and eat your own food.

Maybe some staff use mealtimes to prepare their rooms for the next activity or session. Maybe they are used to the break and even have it scheduled as part of their statutory break time. Perhaps staff don't like the food and don't really want it, preferring to bring their own. They also may not want as many snacks as are appropriate for small children.

Of course, staff preferences need to be respected, especially where there are specific dietary requirements involved. And I am certainly not advocating that staff go without a break! Equally, not all staff may feel that they are able to model a positive relationship with food if they don't have one themselves. That needs to be listened to. Chapter 12 goes into detail about how our own relationship with food can have an impact on the children around us. That is why thinking about your own beliefs and behaviours is so important, so that you can get to grips with what you may be modelling without even realising it.

I recommend that you look very carefully at how and whether it would be possible for staff to eat with the children. At snack time, you could perhaps only take a tiny piece. It doesn't matter how much you actually eat. Maybe you could draw up your rota so that (assuming you meet your required ratios) staff could take it in turns to eat with the children. It is so much easier to create that positive eating environment described in earlier in this section, when you are sitting down with the children (rather than standing, walking around the room or watching them eat). Even if you can only logistically manage to eat with the children for one meal a day, that is still valuable. Communal eating is about community – to fully support positive meal and snack times, sitting down with the children and enjoying the meal alongside them is fantastic practice.

● ● ● ● ● SECTION 6 ●

NUTRITION AND HEALTHY EATING

In this section, we will think about your obligations in relation to the EYFS Framework and Ofsted. We'll be looking at how to teach nutrition – through fun, not fear – and will talk about the delicate balance inherent in fulfilling your responsibilities in a way that supports a positive relationship with food. We will explore the importance of having a food policy and I will suggest some things to think about when developing one.

— Chapter 20 ────────────────────

HEALTHY EATING AND THE EYFS FRAMEWORK

In this chapter, we will be considering your obligations in relation to teaching about healthy eating. You need to know what is expected of you, but you also need to have an awareness of how to meet these obligations in a way that promotes, rather than hinders, a positive relationship with food. In this chapter, we will be looking at what the EYFS Framework says and what Ofsted look for when they inspect a setting.

THE EYFS FRAMEWORK

In the current EYFS Framework, under the prime area of 'physical development', one aspect of the 'health and self-care' learning goal (ELG05) is that:

> Children know the importance for good health of physical exercise, and a healthy diet, and talk about ways to keep healthy and safe.[1]

Let's look specifically at what this means. In early years, children need to learn about the importance of a healthy diet. This means that they need to have a concept of 'health' and an understanding of the relationship between our health and what we eat.

Health is term that we use a lot in everyday speech; it's one of those words that we all think we know the meaning of. But when we try to actually define a 'healthy diet', it gets a bit tricky. One person's idea of health is not the same as another's. Some people argue against the very notion of a food being intrinsically healthy, saying that the most important thing is balance and context. Some people believe that a healthy diet is all about food being prepared from scratch. Other people think it can be reduced to which nutrients we are able to get from our food. Once thing is certain, the relationship between food and health is far from simple:

> Though there has long been interest in the interaction between food and health, it is known today that this interaction is characterized by complexity.[2]

As an early years practitioner, of course your job is not to teach children all about the subtleties of health science, but it can be a confusing area and it's important that you have a clear understanding of what your responsibilities are.

OFSTED

When Ofsted inspectors visit a setting, one of the things they are looking for as part of the new Common Inspection Framework[3] is evidence of children gaining knowledge of the importance of a healthy diet. In the evaluation schedule used by inspectors[4] (how early years settings will be judged), the 'outstanding' grade descriptor in relation to this is '[Practitioners] are very effective in supporting children's growing understanding of how to keep themselves safe and healthy.' The descriptor for 'good' is: 'Practitioners give clear messages to children about why it is important to have a healthy diet and the need for physical exercise, while providing these things within the setting.'

It is important to be able to evidence a 'whole setting approach to exercise and healthy eating'.[5] Children need to understand the significance of what they eat in relation to their health, in an age-appropriate way. But this is not knowledge to be held in isolation; these messages have to be embedded in the daily life of a setting, with healthy eating being an integral part of the provision. Additionally, not only do children need to know about how to keep themselves healthy, they must also learn to 'make healthy choices in relation to food'.[6]

LOOKING AT YOUR PROVISION

The Children's Food Trust have created (in partnership with Action4) a fantastic guide for early years settings in England called *Promoting and*

Supporting Healthy Eating in Early Years Settings.[7] This guide includes a set of questions for staff to ask themselves, in order to think about whether they are fulfilling their duties in relation to promoting and supporting healthy eating. This is both in terms of what is taught to children and the food that is provided. It includes links to further resources and is free to download from the Children's Food Trust website.

As we have seen so far in this book, food is an emotive subject. Children may not be confident eaters and they may not have had much opportunity to access a varied diet. Many young children are picky eaters and obesity is a growing problem in our pre-school population. All of this means that messages about healthy eating and nutrition need to be delivered extremely thoughtfully. When a health agenda is pursued in a way that could be seen as heavy-handed, it is possible to actually damage a child's relationship with food: to make their eating worse. In the next chapter, we will be looking at practical ways to make sure that messages about healthy eating are conveyed in a positive and psychologically healthy way.

Chapter 21

FUN NOT FEAR
How to teach about nutrition

We are now going to build on what we covered in the previous chapter, about understanding your obligations in terms of the EYFS Framework (in relation to supporting healthy eating). In this chapter, we are going to explore how to approach ELG05 in a way that promotes a positive relationship with food.

USE POSITIVE LANGUAGE

If you look closely at the language used around diet, you will see that some food groups are often demonised. Nutrition messages may be shared with a heavily moral overtone, often with a lot of negativity. For example, 'Sugar will rot your teeth' or 'You shouldn't eat white bread.' These are very absolute statements and they have a threatening tone. Young children are open and trusting – they also see the world in black and white. For example, if an adult tells them that white bread is bad for them, they may well go home feeling frightened and guilty because white bread is what they have for breakfast every day.

Make sure whenever you communicate a message about nutrition and health, you couch it in positive terms. For example, rather than teaching that white bread is 'bad for us', tell children how great whole grains are for our bodies. Rather than using the moral imperative 'should' – for example, 'You should eat fruit' – talk about nutrition in terms of what our bodies need: 'Our bodies need all the goodness we get from fruit.'

Make 'we' statements, like 'we only have sweets occasionally because too much sugar isn't very good for our health', instead of saying 'you mustn't have too many sweets'. Put simply, every time you convey a message about nutrition, ask yourself whether you have described it in terms of a behaviour – 'what we do' because of 'what our bodies need' – rather than in negative, moralistic terms.

BE CAREFUL HOW YOU DELIVER HEALTH MESSAGES WHILE CHILDREN ARE EATING

The best place to teach about nutrition is not at mealtimes. This sounds counter-intuitive because, while the food is in front of us, it may feel like a natural time to bring this topic up. However, it is very hard to talk about nutrition while eating without slipping into controlling approaches to feeding (see Section 2). It's great to model thinking about health, for example by eating your apple and saying 'this is so crunchy and tasty and also full of the vitamins my body needs!'. But be very careful that you don't use your duty to teach children about health, as a way of trying to get them to eat or drink certain things.

This is a subtle point, because you do need to teach children about making healthy choices. However, using nutrition as a way of rationalising with a child in order to persuade them to eat something is a controlling feeding practice. Consider the difference between these two scenarios: Charlie has decided he doesn't want his banana at snack time because it's slimy. The adult tells him to try it because it's full of very important nutrients and will give him the energy he needs for the rest of the morning. This may be true, but you are taking on Charlie's job of deciding what he is going to eat in the context of what is provided (see Chapter 3).

In the second scenario, the children are all sitting enjoying a banana and you share some fun banana facts. The first could be that monkeys peel them upside-down! The second could be that they are full of a special mineral (potassium) which helps our hearts to beat. The third could be that bananas float if you put them in water. If the children are enthusiastic, you could even demonstrate this last one, or watch a video of monkeys peeling bananas and try to copy them. This illustration shows how positive, fun messages which are not connected to children's eating are a great way to teach about nutrition with a light touch.

It is worth noting that rational arguments for eating are rarely successful when working with picky eaters. This is because if a child is genuinely anxious about trying something new or disliked, that anxiety is so much more powerful than any motivation they may have, based on the nutritional benefit of that food. Children live in the present and are not motivated by long-term gain.

If Charlie is pressured to try his banana, he will probably have a negative experience. Next time he sees a banana, he'll remember that and his dislike will have been reinforced. If he is allowed to simply explore his banana without eating it, maybe smelling it and handling it as he sits with the other children, he has come a tiny step closer to accepting and getting to know bananas.

Encouraging children to eat because something is good for them may be culturally normal, but it does not support a positive relationship with food. You can encourage a child to eat good food by having great quality food in your setting, by giving children lots of positive experiences with food, and by using all the other good practice described in this book. This goes back to the notion of a whole setting approach to healthy eating. Genuinely embedded, 'lived' good practice will help children make healthy choices. Promoting healthy eating does not mean telling children to eat their cabbage because otherwise they won't grow big and strong.

TEACH ABOUT BALANCE

Rather than conveying the idea that foods are either 'goodies' or 'baddies', talk about balance. There are lots of resources available to support teaching about a balanced diet, such as the government Eatwell Guide (see the Resources section for details). You can explain that there are some foods which we only eat occasionally and some foods we need often. Talking about biology and illustrating some of the things we need different nutrients for is a great way of helping children to understand the concept that we need foods from different groups. This physical rather than moral argument for a balanced and varied diet helps children feel good about eating rather than fearful or guilty. The most positive message you can convey is that we need to try our best to enjoy a balanced diet which is full of fresh, wholesome food, cooked from scratch.

EMBED MESSAGES ABOUT HEALTHY EATING INTO THE CURRICULUM

The best way to teach children about healthy eating is to embed it into your planning (see the Resources section for support for planning). For example, rather than delivering a 'white bread is bad for you' message, visit a windmill, learning about the benefits of whole grains in our diet. Bake some bread with the children. Teach them to choose whole grains whenever they can, while remembering that many of them may not have those opportunities outside your setting. It is essential never to shame children for the food they have at home.

You can kill two birds with one stone by engaging children with where their food comes from – perhaps through visits to a farm if you have access to one, or through gardening – while also teaching them about what their bodies need. Make it fun, positive and interactive, all the things you will already be great at, as an early years practitioner.

DON'T BURDEN CHILDREN WITH TOO MUCH RESPONSIBILITY FOR THEIR DIET

Ultimately, it is the adult's job to decide what foods are available, both at home and at the setting a child attends. You have an obligation to help children to learn about making healthy choices, and this will come indirectly from the kinds of good practice described above. The way to promote better eating at home is through working with parents (see Section 7) because they are the ones who make the choices about what food they provide.

A child attending a setting where good practice is genuinely embedded will be unconsciously learning about making healthy choices every day. They will hopefully take what they have learned with them as they grow older and start to have more direct responsibility for the content of their diet. It is too much to expect of a four-year-old, for example, that they would be offered sweets at home and decline. Bringing in guilt about eating, at such a young age, is really unhelpful. You can convey messages about how we have sugary foods occasionally and we need a balanced diet, but it's important to be very conscious of not making children feel responsible if they are given unhealthy food at home.

BE CAREFUL TO AVOID SHAMING CHILDREN

When children talk about eating something that may not be perceived as healthy, like fast food, don't make them feel bad about it. If they bring things to school in their lunch box, make sure that if there is a problem with what they have brought, you take this up with their parents not them. There have been many anecdotal examples of children being shamed for the contents of their lunch box – staff pouring sweet drinks down the sink, or taking away a chocolate bar. These kinds of practices can be mortifying for a child and very confusing too.

If the children at your setting bring food in from home, make sure you have clear guidelines in your food policy about what you consider acceptable. Make sure changes you ask for are achievable – not all parents are confident when it comes to changing the food they provide. Affordability may be an issue to. Take a supportive stance and do what you can to work with parents and try to understand their concerns. You can learn more about this in the next chapter, all about your food policy.

Chapter 22

YOUR FOOD POLICY

Although there are some statutory EYFS policies, a food policy is not one of them. However, I would argue that it is good practice to have a food policy which is used to convey the setting's approach to food provision and learning about food, as it is an effective way of making sure that the children are receiving consistent messages about healthy eating.

The Children's Food Trust provides both a policy template and step-by-step guide to developing a food policy in consultation with staff, children and parents, which you could consider when you write your policy.[1] They also have a suggested code of practice which you can adopt.[2]

CREATING A FOOD POLICY

If you have a food policy:

- you can refer to it when you explain to parents and carers why you approach food in certain ways when they register with your setting

- you can make sure practices are consistent across all staff

- you will be demonstrating that food is a priority for you and that you follow best practice.

Dr Patricia Mucavele, of the Children's Food Trust, explains the purpose of a food policy:

A food policy is used to convey the setting's approach to food provision and learning about food, and is an effective way of making sure that the children are receiving consistent messages about healthy eating. Policies can include information on the setting's approach to the food and drink provided; how the setting communicates about food with children and families; a description of the eating environment and social aspects of meal times; the types of food provided as part of celebrations and special events; and how the setting caters for cultural, religious and special dietary requirements, including managing allergies and intolerances. It can also guide parents on the types of food and drink which can be bought in from home, the importance of breastfeeding, having a healthy weight, and good dental health. The policy can also convey how children learn about, and through food, the setting's food safety and hygiene procedures, and its approach to staff food, nutrition and hygiene training.[3]

In order to create a food policy which can be genuinely embedded and is not just a 'pen and paper exercise', you need to consider its development carefully. Here are some suggestions about things to think about when writing a food policy:

1. What is your vision for how food and feeding are managed in your setting? What are your aims? Are there any core principles you want everyone to know about?

2. Can you communicate a concise and thought-out rationale for your aims and vision?

3. How does your vision in relation to food fit in with your setting's wider vision and strategy?

4. How can you consult stakeholders? Involving parents and staff will give everyone a sense of ownership of the policy, helping them engage with and support it.

5. Can you carry out an audit to support the development of your food policy? You could look at areas such as what foods are brought in from home, or how many parents perceive issues like picky eating or weight to be a problem for their child.

6. How will your food policy dovetail with relevant key obligations, like keeping children safe, equality and inclusion?

7. How will you communicate with parents about what food and drink is made available to their child? This is one of your obligations listed in the EYFS Statutory Framework (2017).[4]

8. Who will your key staff members be in relation to food and what are their responsibilities?

9. If you allow food to be brought in from home in your setting, are you very clear about your expectations? Can you communicate what steps will be taken if those expectations are not met?

10. Have you articulated how you manage picky eating?

11. Have you articulated how you support specific dietary requirements, including those with a religious or cultural basis, as well as allergies and intolerances?

12. How will you be monitoring and evaluating the effectiveness of your policy?

LIFTING THE LID ON LUNCH BOXES

No discussion of food policies would be complete without a consideration of whether it is good practice to control what children bring in from home in their packed lunch. In 2015, the press reported that the Parliamentary Under Secretary of State for Schools, Lord Nash (answering a question in the House of Lords), stated that teachers can legally 'confiscate, keep or destroy' food items which they deem to be unhealthy. He added that: 'If schools wish to adopt such policies, we strongly recommend that they consult parents first and ensure that any adopted policy is clearly communicated to parents and pupils.'[5] Lord Nash's comments came in the wake of strong opinions being expressed by parents of pupils at Cherry Tree Primary School in Colchester, after food items – allegedly including a scotch egg – were confiscated by staff. Lord Nash emphasised that it is up to an individual governing body whether or not they decide to ban certain foods in the interests of promoting a healthy diet.

This is a thorny issue. Let's start with the aspects of it that I would argue should not be up for debate. First, it is never a good idea to impose restrictions without this being clearly communicated in your food policy in the first instance. Second, it is never appropriate to shame a child for the contents of their lunch box, as discussed in the previous chapter.

The School Food Plan[6] is a set of recommendations produced by restaurateurs Henry Dimbleby and John Vincent, published by the DfES in 2013. In it, the authors suggest that schools might want to enforce a ban on unhealthy foods being brought in from home. They list sugary drinks, crisps and confectionary as items to ban. They also suggest giving children incentives for bringing in healthy packed lunches.[7] It is worth noting that the scope of this document does not extend to the early years sector. However, it is still relevant as a barometer of official opinion on food brought in from home.

I believe that every setting needs to make a decision that feels right for them in terms of their requirements regarding packed lunches. However, I have some reservations about Vincent and Dimbleby's suggestions. An outright ban that is imposed through confiscating or destroying food brought in by children seems to me to potentially do more harm than good.

Indeed, this was the opinion expressed by a school included in the report as an example of good practice: a primary school in Bristol felt that the potential negative impact of a ban (on the relationship between the school and parents) was not worth risking. Instead, they sent home weekly newsletters reminding parents of their guidelines and including information about why the guidelines were in place. For example, 'Jam or chocolate spread sandwiches do not have the necessary protein to support children's learning throughout the afternoon.'[8]

This is perhaps a workable compromise. Schools and early years settings will want to promote and support a healthy diet. However, many parents feel strongly that it is their right to make their own decisions about what goes into children's lunch boxes. The anger and hostility than a ban may provoke could make working with parents much harder in the long run.

I suggest including guidelines in your food policy rather than imposing an outright ban. If children repeatedly bring in foods that are not in keeping with your guidelines, rather than remove those foods – which is humiliating for the child – perhaps have a standard note to go home to parents reminding them of your guidelines. It is better to take an educational rather than judgemental tone, explaining the basis for your guidelines and treating parents with respect. It is also worth noting that if a child is repeatedly sent to school with food that will not meet their nutritional needs or is inadequate, this may need to be considered from a child protection perspective.

It is very important that any guidelines you share in relation to the contents of lunchboxes, are good quality and evidence-based. Make sure they are in line with the Children's Food Trust Voluntary Guidelines on food and drink. Look at the 'Food brought in from home' section of their Voluntary Guidelines.[9] The table showing examples of suitable food and drink is especially helpful and could be shared with parents. The Children's Food Trust has also produced a fantastic leaflet all about healthy packed lunches for early years.[10]

I have some concerns about the notion of incentivising children for bringing in a healthy packed lunch. Ultimately, it is parents and not children who have control over what goes into a lunch box. This is especially true in the context of early years. I would argue that rewarding children for bringing in healthy food is a way of discriminating against those whose parents are perhaps less educated and know less about nutrition and food preparation, or maybe cannot afford a wider variety of healthy food. Equally, some parents who have a chaotic lifestyle or issues like poor mental health to contend with may find it hard to consistently provide a healthy, balanced packed lunch. Do we really want to make our most vulnerable children feel inadequate because of what is in their lunch boxes?

SOME SUGGESTIONS IN RELATION TO PACKED LUNCHES

- Make sure that if you decide to impose a ban on certain foods, you clearly indicate what these foods are and why you are banning them, in your food policy. Arbitrary or inconsistent banning of foods is extremely bad practice.

- If you decide to ban certain items, consider letting the child have them that day, then sending a note home, rather than shaming the child and leaving them hungry because you have confiscated their food.

- In the case of very picky eaters (see Section 9), make allowances in your food policy enabling them to bring in their safe foods from home. This needs to be done at the setting's discretion, on a case by case basis. It is not an excuse for all children to deviate from your guidelines. It is an assurance that children who accept a very limited range of foods can have their needs met, while families and staff work together to help them access a more varied diet.

- Consider taking a positive and informative perspective on packed lunches, sending home ideas and nutritional information while reminding parents of your guidelines. This is less likely to damage the parent–staff relationship than an authoritarian, critical stance.

- If you can access appropriate expertise (and have the resources), support parents in providing nutritious and varied food by offering training opportunities.

WORKING WITH PARENTS

In this section, we will think about effective working with parents and just how far practitioners' responsibilities extend. We will look at how parents can feel judged and criticised, as well as how to avoid contributing to this. The last two chapters in this section focus on the kinds of skills we need to help children develop in relation to eating and drinking, and how to work with parents towards this end.

BEING A TEAM

In this chapter, we'll be thinking about why it is so important to work effectively with parents in order to support children's relationship with food. We'll be looking at how to distinguish between what is your responsibility as a setting, and what is beyond your control.

CONSISTENCY

Children eat several times a day. Each of those meals or snacks can be seen as a tiny window of opportunity to nurture a child's relationship with food. But however fantastic your food policy, and however well-informed your staff or colleagues, what a child experiences when they attend your setting is only a small fragment of the picture. A child's life at home, day in, day out, has a significant role to play.

You will have seen many instances of work you have done with children not being supported (or perhaps even being contradicted) at home. Maybe you have spent a long time helping a child gain in independence, putting on their own shoes or hanging up their own coat, only to find that this is not replicated in the home environment. This is not to blame or criticise parents; families are dealing with all sorts of pressures and their child putting on their own coat may not be a top priority. However, as a practitioner, if you can do whatever is within your power to ensure that strategies used in your setting are supported at home, that consistency will be of enormous benefit to the child.

HOW CAN SETTINGS FOSTER CONSISTENCY?

Ensure communication is good

Great communication is an essential part of working well with parents. If parents don't feel able to talk to you (or don't feel heard by you) you will not have the makings of a good team. Good communication is important for all aspects of a child's education and development, not just their relationship with food. Parents need to feel welcome at your setting, so that they can comfortably come in for a chat. They need to have many opportunities to speak to staff, whether that is when they drop off or collect their child, or in other contexts like parents' coffee mornings. They need to feel you have time to listen and that you are likely to be receptive and understanding.

Have clear expectations

If you want the good practice you strive for in your setting to be supported at home, your expectations need to be clear and reasonable. If you have only communicated a vague notion of what parents can do to support your work – or given no guidance at all – it is likely that families will not be on the same page as you. Make sure you communicate in plain English (and provide translation where applicable), avoiding jargon. It is also important to ensure that the whole staff team reiterate the same messages so there is no room for confusion. An effective food policy (see Chapter 22) will help you communicate clear and consistent expectations.

Make goals realistic

If a child appears to lack eating skills or to have a dysfunctional relationship with food, rather than swamp their parent with lots of information, pick one or two key things to work on in the first instance. You can build on these over time. As a parent, it can feel that you are being told you're getting it all wrong. It can also feel overwhelming if you are given too much information at once. For example, if a child never eats at a table, never uses cutlery and always has the television on during meals, the first step could be supporting parents in getting a child used to eating at the table, before even considering introducing cutlery or suggesting no screens during meals.

Use multiple opportunities to share good practice with parents

If parents are used to coming into your setting and working with you to learn about what you do and how they can help, you already have the makings of a fantastic team. There are so many ways to share, and you are probably doing lots of these already. You can invite parents in to talk to them about how you teach phonics. You can invite them in to show them a display of the children's' artwork or to watch a performance the children have prepared. You can invite them to join in with cultural activities like trying new foods for Chinese New Year, for example. If parents are used to visiting your setting to learn and to celebrate the children's achievements, they are likely to be much more open to coming in when you invite them to talk about something sensitive, like food.

Have written guidelines to promote key messages

As well as your food policy, it is a good idea to prepare some accessible written information for parents to keep, or alternatively, to pass on resources obtained from a trusted source. You will find some great sources of information in the resource guide.

WHAT IS WITHIN YOUR REMIT?

This is a question that goes to the heart of the relationship between parents and settings, and applies to much more than just food. Is it for you to tell parents to toilet train children? Is it your right to suggest that a family should eat a healthier diet? Does your responsibility end once a child walks out of your door? The line here is blurry, and you will make your decisions in this regard based on the ethos of your setting and the needs of your parent community.

Let's explore the two extremes of this grey area in order to reflect on where the boundary lies. First, if a practitioner believes a child is being neglected (for example, not given enough food to eat) or is at risk of neglect, there is a clear child protection protocol which they are obliged to follow. At the other end of the scale, if a parent were giving a child sweets on their walk home from pre-school every day, a practitioner may not approve of that, but it is not really their role to tell the parent to stop doing it because personal freedom needs to be acknowledged.

Here are some questions to ask yourself when you are considering whether a child's eating behaviour falls within your remit.

Does it have an impact on how that child is when they attend the setting?

For example, if a child comes into school every day extremely hungry, to the point that they are unable to happily take part in activities until they have had their morning snack, you may want to chat with their parent about breakfast. Perhaps that parent explains that mornings are too chaotic to fit breakfast in. You could talk with them about possible strategies to surmount this. It's relevant to that child's behaviour at your setting.

Maybe a child only ever asks for pasta during school lunches, and you invite their parent in to talk about this. It could be that this is all they are served at home, so home habits are impacting the choices that child makes at your setting. If you provide a variety of healthy foods and that child isn't accessing it, this becomes something you can work with parents to address. It's relevant to that child's experience of your provision.

If a child is unable to sit at the table and use cutlery, or is upset at mealtimes because they are used to eating with the television on, this has an impact on that child that is relevant to you. You will have certain expectations about how communal meals will be (set out in your food policy) and if a child struggles with these, it is good practice to work with their family and see how you can best support that child.

Let's look back at the example of the child who is given sweets every day on the way home from pre-school. You may not approve of this, but does it have an impact on that child accessing your provision? Does it affect their behaviour while they attend your setting? Probably not. If you have the resources and expertise, it's great to offer educational sessions around healthy lifestyle for parents, including information about sugar. However, that's very different from making specific judgements about individual choices.

Is there a referral you should be making?

When you are thinking about what falls within your remit, part of that question has to be about whether a child or family needs support which is beyond what you can offer. If a child's eating is very limited, you may suggest a referral to the school nurse. If you are very concerned about a child's health, you may suggest parents visit their GP or health visitor. If you have concerns about a child's behaviour, you may decide to refer this to the special educational needs coordinator (SENCO) if you are in a school context. As always, if you suspect a child may be at risk of harm, you must follow your child protection policy.

Is help being sought?

If a child's issues don't merit a referral and parents are adamant that they don't want your support, forcing the issue may damage your relationship with that parent and could potentially make it harder for you to work well with them in the long run. For example, if a child doesn't eat any fruit in your setting or at home, parents may not see that as a problem. Having shared information and offered support, there is not much you can do if it is refused.

As we will see in the next chapter, feeding is an extremely emotive and sensitive subject; there are all sorts of reasons why parents can feel a bit defensive. Sometimes, a family may not wish to come in and see you to talk about their child's eating, but they might attend an educational session open to all parents. Sharing good quality information about how to help children develop a good relationship with food and enjoy a healthy lifestyle is always positive.

- Chapter 24 ———————————————————

EMPOWERING
WITHOUT BLAMING

Before we look at some practical ways to work with families to support a positive relationship with food, let's think about why children's eating can be such a sensitive subject. Speaking as a mum myself, parents have a strong urge to nurture their children. Feeding them is a huge part of this. It begins at birth, when a baby needs their parent to feed them in order to ensure their survival. If parents didn't have an overwhelming instinct to feed their children, that would jeopardise the very continuation of the human race. This instinct is incredibly powerful.

It is important not to make gender assumptions, because families come in many different configurations. However, in my clinical experience, it is often mothers who most powerfully feel this urge to feed children 'successfully'. And when things go wrong in relation to feeding, they are often the ones who experience this with the most emotional force. I have heard mothers of children who are underweight, overweight or are just very limited eaters, talk about a profound sense of failure and guilt.

These difficult emotions and critical judgements of the self are felt at an individual level. However, everything has a social context. Our values and beliefs are culturally informed and we need to look at the messages society sends to parents as well as how they feel about themselves. Indeed, the two things are intrinsically linked.

The construct of 'mother-blaming' describes how factors like children's health status may be 'blamed' on mothers. Researchers writing about mother-blaming say:

As mothers, the behaviour and actions of women are subject to scrutiny in ways that men, as fathers, are not, and these behaviours and actions are often linked to family and child health outcomes in the way that male activities are not.[1]

As a practitioner, you might be seeing a child's eating issues in an objective way, thinking predominantly about what that child's needs may be. The child's parent, however, might not hear objective advice – what they may hear is criticism and judgement, coloured by what they are told by society and perhaps what their own inner-critic believes.

Always assume that food will be a highly sensitive topic and tread extremely carefully. A focus on listening, taking a compassionate stance and providing evidence-based information will facilitate this. All of these things are good practice regardless of what you are supporting parents with, and these will no doubt be skills you already use day to day.

LISTENING

If a parent has concerns about their child's eating, or if you have raised concerns with them, take time to really hear their perspective. Feeding issues can be extremely complex and you need to give parents time and space to express their thoughts and feelings about the problem. Only once you have done that can you begin to work together to support their child.

Make time for a meeting dedicated to talking about their child's relationship with food. Carefully consider how you can support any positive strategies already being used at home, as well as how parents can support the work you are doing with that child in your setting. Plan in a review meeting so that you can monitor progress. It is important to see parents as people you can collaborate with in the child's best interest.

COMPASSION

Parents so often feel judged when it comes to their child's eating. Make sure you are kind, compassionate and don't convey any sense of blame. It can be useful to let parents know that food issues are relatively common (see the stats on picky eating and obesity in their respective chapters). This is not to minimise anyone's concerns, but if a family is worrying, it is very helpful for them to understand that they are not alone. There is such a stigma around these problems and helping parents see that they are grappling with a challenge that others are also facing can help foster a positive, problem-solving attitude rather than a sense of shame.

EVIDENCE-BASED INFORMATION

Eating is something that we all do – it is part of the fabric of life. Anything that forms part of our everyday experience develops its own set of clichés and myths. It is very important to avoid repeating clichés and make sure that any food-related advice you give has a sound basis. For example, parents often report being told that eventually, even the pickiest child will eat when they are hungry enough. The 'they won't starve' mantra is extremely unhelpful and, in many cases, it is untrue. This cliché has caused a huge amount of stress for both the parents who have tried to follow it and the children in their care. Children whose eating is very limited feel such intense anxiety about eating certain foods that they will go without anything for very long periods of time, rather than eat something that is too difficult for them. Childhood eating problems have many complex causes[2] and writing picky eating off as a battle of wills that the adult needs to win is very unhelpful.

BE CLEAR ABOUT YOUR ROLE

We looked at the question of what falls within your remit in the previous chapter. This is intrinsically linked to how you define your role. In order to maintain appropriate boundaries, I suggest conceptualising your role as follows. Your tasks are to:

- get a clear picture of the problem

- explore how good practice already happening at home can be replicated at your setting

- explore how you can share approaches used in your setting with parents, so it can be replicated at home

- make sure you have made any appropriate referrals and have taken advice from your line manager or the SENCO where applicable, following your setting's protocols.

It is not your job to be that child's therapist, nurse or social worker and an essential part of effective and ethical practice is knowing the limits to the help you can provide. If you understand your core goal as striving for consistency across home and your setting, this fosters clarity around the level of support you can offer.

CONSISTENCY

It is so important that feeding issues are approached consistently. If children get one message at home and another at the setting they attend, this will be confusing and will slow their progress. For example, if a child's eating behaviours are being responded to with lots of attention at home, they may continue to look for this attention via their eating behaviours when they are at pre-school.

Equally, replicating an approach that is being used at home, which you don't believe is good practice, is problematic. For example, many parents employ controlling feeding tactics if they are worried their child is overweight (see Chapter 38). There is clear research evidence which shows that this is harmful. If parents want you to do things which you don't believe are in a child's best interest, explain the rationale for your position as clearly as possible. You may also be able to refer to your food policy if you have one. Unless you are concerned that parents' choices pose a risk to a child, there is nothing you can do about what happens at home beyond sharing evidence-based information and doing your best to maintain good communication with that family.

UNDERSTANDING EATING SKILLS

Eating comprises a set of skills to be learnt. We are not born knowing how to do it…in fact, these skills are built gradually over time and some children will have missed out on certain aspects of this, by the time they come to you. In this chapter, we're going to break down some key eating skills in order to think about how we can support children in acquiring them. We will conclude this chapter with a look at how to work with parents to support children's eating skills.

SITTING AT A TABLE

Sitting at a table may not seem like a skill, but for some children it is really hard, especially those who may not be used to sitting at a table for meals at home. It can also be tricky for children who are very picky eaters and have negative feelings about mealtimes. You will have a strong sense of how easy the children in your care find it to concentrate more generally. Attention spans vary greatly, and for children who are not good at staying in one place for a long time, sitting at the table can be a struggle.

The influence of peers can have a very positive effect in this regard, because most children will want to be at the table, where the action is, along with their friends. However, if a child is finding sitting at a table very challenging, help them learn to do this gradually. Slowly increase the length of time you expect them to sit at the table so that you are setting them up to succeed. If they only manage one extra minute at each meal for a week, before building in two extra minutes the next week, this is still real progress. This gentle approach is much better than having a battle with that child every day. Use plenty of positive reinforcement and praise and give them visual cues (like a sand timer) to help them understand your expectations.

Sitting comfortably?

Make sure that you have the optimum seating arrangements in place, because problems in this area can make it very hard for children to sit at the table and can exacerbate eating issues.

Here are some things to check for:

- Can children sit with their feet firmly on the ground (or on a stool or similar)?

- Do their chairs offer good back support so they can sit up straight without straining?

- Do they have enough space, so they don't feel squashed?

- Is the table the right height for them?

- Do they look relaxed at the table or are they tense, making an effort to support themselves?

- Is there a 90-degree angle at their ankle, knee and hip?

Consider using cushions or rolled up towels to give children extra support if this is required, although ideally in an early years setting, appropriate chairs and tables should be available.

USING CUTLERY

Most babies can manage self-feeding and have a go with a soft spoon at around 12 months. Many begin earlier than that. The NHS 'Birth to five development timeline'[1] states that children begin to learn how to use a knife and fork between the ages of three and five. I think it is helpful to think of these skills developing over this 24-month period. However, children vary greatly, both in terms of their fine motor skills and what they will have been exposed to at home.

It is important to support self-feeding for toddlers and pre-schoolers, and some children may come to you expecting to be fed by an adult. It can become (or perhaps is at home) part of a power dynamic where a child gets attention because eating is dependent on an adult being next to them and physically putting the food in their mouth. Sometimes, parents excessively infantilise children or are not aware of normal developmental trajectories, and feed a child way beyond babyhood. This can also be a strategy used by parents of picky eaters. Unless a child's special educational needs or disability (SEND) merits help with feeding, this can be extremely problematic and you need to gently help those children learn to feed themselves.

If a child is used to eating everything with their fingers, there are a few things to think about when you consider how best to nurture appropriate independent eating skills. First, is this age appropriate? Second, may there be a more general developmental delay or an underlying condition which could explain the way they eat? If a child has SEND, their eating must be understood through this lens and expectations need to be tailored to that individual child.

Third, how is that child's relationship with food? If a child is not relaxed and happy during mealtimes, this needs to be addressed before you look at their eating skills. Putting pressure on a child (for example, to use a knife and fork) when they are already anxious or struggling with the communal eating situation, will make their eating worse. We need to remember Maslow's hierarchy of needs.[2] The most basic needs must be met before we can move on to the higher order needs. In this context, that means that a child must first be able to sit at a table and happily take part in communal meal and snack times. Only then can we can begin to build their eating skills.

The same principle applies to the way in which we introduce cutlery, both to younger children who may be learning to self-feed for the first time, and to older children who lack age-appropriate eating skills. The following steps are a guide to the stages of supporting cutlery use. Make sure each skill has been mastered before focusing on the next stage.

1. A child is happy to sit at the table and take part in communal meals and snacks.

2. A child is able to self-feed without utensils.

3. A child is able to self-feed with a soft spoon.

4. A child is able to self-feed with a metal spoon.

5. A child is able to self-feed with a fork.

6. A child is able to use a fork in their non-dominant hand.

7. A child is able to hold a knife (without using it) in their dominant hand while using the fork in their other hand to eat.

8. A child is able to do both a sawing motion (e.g. chopping a carrot) and a pushing motion (moving food towards the fork with their knife) with their knife.

9. A child uses a knife and fork to eat, simultaneously.

The stage where children simply hold a knife in their dominant hand (not using it) while eating with the fork in their other hand, is often missed out. However, it is a huge leap to move from just using a fork, to coordinating two hands, especially when children are also being asked to swap the fork from their right to left hand. Children often need to stay at this stage for a while, and can move on to actually using the knife once they can cope easily with holding both a knife and a fork at the same time.

It is worth noting that you will already have a good idea about a child's fine motor skills. If you feel that a child's problems with cutlery stem from a more general delay in motor skill development, you will no doubt have many ways of developing these in non-food related contexts. Another important consideration is making sure you have appropriate cutlery. If we had to eat with giant knives and forks, we would certainly find this hard!

We need to tread a fine line between helping children develop age-appropriate eating skills, on one hand, and being excessively focused on manners, on the other. If knife and fork use become too central a priority, this can lead to a tense atmosphere where children feel anxious and criticised. As with every aspect of eating, the core goal must always be getting the environment right (see Chapter 17). Once this is in place, we can gently work to build children's skills and independence.

TOLERATING HUNGER

As described in the first section of this book, children need to be able to cope with appropriate hunger, and to recognise the physical cues that constitute appetite. If children have been fed in a grazing pattern, or if they are given (or help themselves to) snacks on demand at home, feeling a bit hungry before a meal can be very difficult and may be an unusual feeling for them.

We can help them by modelling listening to our bodies' cues (for example, saying, 'My tummy is aching a bit, I wonder if my body is telling me it's nearly time for lunch?') and by giving them the names for their sensations. So, if a child often says they have a tummy ache and you are confident that they are experiencing feelings of hunger that they cannot recognise (and are not unwell!), tell them, 'You are hungry – your body is ready for food.' You can also explain that these feelings are okay and we all feel this way for a short while before we eat, just as we feel full afterwards.

Displaying a visual reminder of meal and snack times – perhaps pictures of the week's menu or a pictorial timetable – is a great way of helping children who find it hard to wait for food. If they feel hungry, pointing out that snack time will happen after outdoor play, for example, is very reassuring and will help children learn to self-regulate. It is much easier to tolerate hunger if we know when our food is coming.

If a child is coming to your setting hungry because they have not had enough to eat at home, this needs to be addressed on a case by case basis, with reference to your child protection policy. It is very important to understand that hunger born of neglect is not acceptable, but hunger in the context of appropriate food being provided at appropriate times is part of the rhythm of the day.

WORKING WITH PARENTS

It is great practice to share with parents some of your expectations in terms of eating skills. Here are a few ways to work with parents to boost eating skills:

- Run a session on eating skills as part of your induction, so that parents understand your expectations before their child starts at your setting.

- Although it is not a statutory requirement, in some areas practitioners will carry out a home visit in the Summer term before a child joins their school reception class. If this if this is something you do, it is a good idea to use this opportunity to talk about eating skills and any food-related concerns parents may have.

- Hold an 'Eating Q & A' session for parents, where you can offer general advice and answer questions about your food policy and how meal and snack times work at your setting.

- Invite parents into your setting to have a meal with the children, before their child starts, so they can get an insight into how you run meal and snack times.

- Prepare or source written resources to share with parents, giving information on how eating skills can be supported at home.

• Chapter 26 ———————————————————————

ALL ABOUT DRINKING

Having looked at eating skills in the last chapter, we're now going to consider fluids. This is an area where parental support can be an essential part of helping children develop healthy skills and habits. The recommendation for drink provision in the voluntary food and drink guidelines for early years settings in England, (produced by the Child Food Trust)[1] is that the only drinks provided between meals and with snacks should be water and milk. Fruit juice (concentrate and fresh juice, as opposed to squash) should only be provided with meals (not snacks) and should be diluted so that it is 50 per cent water. All other soft drinks (including 'fruit juice drinks' and squash) should be avoided. The guide also states that children should be able to access water at all times and should be encouraged to help themselves to water.

MILK

The Nursery Milk Scheme[2] is operated on the behalf of the Department of Health in the UK. It entitles all children under the age of five, who attend approved day care facilities, to a third of a pint of milk (free of charge) every day. A setting needs to be registered with Ofsted (or equivalent) in order to seek approval for this scheme. Milk is a valuable source of nutrients and this free provision is extremely beneficial for children's health at a national level.

A case study at a nursery class attached to a primary school in West London[3] found that parents' uptake of free milk was not as high as it could be. Although the nursery in this case study allowed children to bring in drinks from home which would not be permitted by settings following current guidance, it still contains valuable lessons for early years practitioners, including implications for training.

These include making the ritual of giving children milk as appealing as possible, by using attractive (potentially personalised) cups or pouring it into a jug. Children could be involved in collecting and counting the milk. Practitioners should be mindful of the kind of language they use around drinks and the beginning and end of sessions should be used to have informal discussions with parents about nutrition and health, alongside more formal talks.

USING AN OPEN CUP

It is culturally normal for young children to be given cups with spouts for their drinks, and many children may come to your setting with no experience whatsoever of drinking from an open cup. The Children's Food Trust[4] recommend offering children drinks in an open cup, because this is supportive of dental health, as children sip rather than suck the liquid.

Sara Keel, who founded the award-winning company BabyCup because she couldn't find an open cup the right size or made of the right materials for her young children, told me when I interviewed her for an article in 2015[5] that children 'need the suck of a vacuum cleaner' to drink from non-spill cups. She described how this uses different facial muscles from open cup drinking, potentially affecting muscle and bone development and increasing the likelihood of a need for orthodontic work later in life.

She also talked about how open cup drinking affects how children drink; if children drink from a cup with a spout, they are much more likely to take their drink with them as they play, rather than drinking as part of a meal or sitting down with a cup of water. Although constant drinking from a cup with a spout is not an option in most settings, helping a child get used to open cup drinking and promoting it among parents, could reduce the risk of them becoming habituated to always having a sweet drink on hand, at home.

Going back to the principles of working effectively with parents outlined earlier in this section, you need to listen to parents – to try to really understand any resistance there may be to using an open cup. Are they concerned about spills? Are they just replicating social norms because most people give their children 'sippy cups' as a matter of course? Do they believe their child may need to carry a drink with them as they play? Are drinks being used to occupy children, or as a way to manage behaviour?

It is important to be compassionate; to recognise that parents can feel judged and criticised and that for some, life could be far too chaotic to find the energy to address what their child drinks out of. Finally, you need to share evidence-based information, explaining why open cups are better for children. As discussed earlier in this section, be mindful of where your responsibilities begin and end. It falls within your remit to ask parents to support children in learning how to use an open cup if you expect them to use these when they attend your setting. If parents choose not to support this at home however, this is their choice.

HELPING CHILDREN LEARN TO USE AN OPEN CUP

Children can begin to learn to use an open cup from six months of age, although of course, babies will also be having milk from either the breast or bottle at that stage. Here are a few suggestions for helping children develop this important skill:

- Do lots of activities involving pouring water from one receptacle to another, so that children can practise the motor skills involved in managing liquids.

- In warm weather, get children drinking water from open cups outside so that they are not anxious about spillages.

- Role play teddy-bears' picnics where children give the teddies drinks from an open cup, to help them get used to this way of drinking.

- For younger children, a slanted cup with handles can be a great tool to help children transition to open cup drinking.

- Serve a smoothie made from milk or yoghurt and fresh fruit for pudding one day, because children may find this thicker liquid easier to control in an open cup.

WHAT WE CAN DO AWAY FROM THE TABLE

In this section, we will begin by thinking about how to use play as a means of indirectly supporting children's eating. This is especially powerful in relation to teaching about mealtime behaviours and helping children who are sensory sensitive. Next, we move on to consider different ways of getting children engaged with and excited about food, while simultaneously making a wider range of foods familiar to them.

THE POWER OF PLAY

As an early years practitioner, you don't need me to tell you about the importance of facilitating learning through play. Play is the cornerstone of what you do! It is a common misconception that most of the hard work, in relation to supporting children's eating, happens at meals. In fact, there is a huge amount that can be done during other parts of the day. In this chapter, we will explore how play can improve children's relationship with food, starting with a look at manners.

MANNERS

Manners are socially determined norms: expectations about our behaviour. At their best, they support respectful interaction with one another. At their worst, they can be excessively prescriptive and unnecessary. If we focus too heavily on table manners, this can raise levels of anxiety and conflict at mealtimes. As we saw in Chapter 17, this affects children's eating negatively. Where manners are completely ignored, however, children's behaviour towards one another may not be thoughtful and this will also have a negative impact on the eating environment.

As a setting, it is important to determine in advance which manners matter. This way, expectations can be clearly and consistently communicated. Make sure you keep the manners you insist upon to a minimum. It is also important to make sure that expectations reflect the age and stage of the children in your care. For example, it would be unreasonable to expect two-year-olds to chew with their mouths shut, but it would be reasonable to expect them to start to learn about saying 'thank you' when they are given their food.

Once you have developed a simple list of manners (or mealtime behaviours) that you value in your setting, it's time to think creatively about ways of teaching these. Role plays are great, because you can talk about why our behaviours matter and help the children reflect on this without feeling that their own behaviour is under the microscope. For example, you might tell a story of a rabbit who wouldn't share the last carrot with its friends. You could get the children to re-enact the story and talk about how all the rabbits might have felt.

You could arrange a picnic for all the toys to attend, and reflect back the make-believe interaction between the toys, to the children. For example, 'Robert the robot didn't ask anyone to pass him his cup of tea, he just grabbed it! I wonder how the other toys felt!' Or, 'Mr Hedgehog asked really nicely for some cake, he must be thinking about other people's feelings...'

Children will love making mud pies and pretending to serve them out. A mud kitchen is always a huge hit and will be great from a sensory perspective. Children will also have a fantastic time organising a picnic with the play food and inviting the teddies. Providing them with as many opportunities for food-related imaginary play as possible will help them practise and think about how we behave when we eat.

MAKING THE UNFAMILIAR, FAMILIAR

Much of children's hesitation about eating new foods is simply that they are not familiar to them. In the next section, where we look at picky eating in more detail, we will touch on an evolutionary argument for why this might be. You are in a fantastic position because you can help children become familiar with foods they may not have seen before, not just through serving them at your setting, but by incorporating them in opportunities for play. Here are a few ideas for ways to help children become familiar with a wide range of foods:

- Introduce a weekly 'What is it?' day when you show the children a new fruit or vegetable and explore how it looks, smells and feels.

- Have 'Fruity Fridays' as described in Chapter 18.

- Use food in your creative activities, making vegetable prints or vegetable dyes, for example.

- Make your play activities dovetail with your menu, for example, include creating a broccoli forest in your planning the week before you serve broccoli.

- Share picture books featuring unfamiliar vegetables and fruit – research shows that this potentially increases consumption![1]

In the next chapter, which is all about how to engage children with their food, you will be able to learn more about how to help children become more familiar with a wide range of foods, through cooking and gardening with them.

SENSORY PLAY

As discussed elsewhere in this book, sensory processing issues can often underpin a dysfunctional relationship with food, and many picky eaters exhibit a certain degree of sensory sensitivity. Messy play is an integral part of the early years curriculum, and it is incredibly valuable in terms of helping children access a varied diet.

If a child is especially sensory sensitive, try and get a sense of which kinds of sense data are tricky for them and then tailor play opportunities to these areas. Equally, some children simply have a cautious temperament (also a group who are often picky eaters) and don't necessarily have problems with sensory processing. Messy play can be a very good way of building a cautious child's confidence in terms of trying something new and becoming more comfortable experiencing unfamiliar sensations.

Here are a few practical suggestions to support sensory play.

Give children control

It is really important to give a child who is a bit unsure about a tactile experience, a measure of control over what they are exposed to. For example, if a child finds it very difficult to tolerate sticky substances on their skin, give them a flannel or some baby wipes so they can wipe their skin when the sensation becomes too much for them. If they are sensitive to smells and you give them a selection of scents to sniff, let them choose how many they have a go at smelling. If they feel out of control, this will raise anxiety.

Babysteps

A common mistake made by adults wanting to help a child with tactile sensitivity, is to jump in at the deep end, assuming that any messy play is going to help a sensitive child. The best path to take, however, is a stepped approach where you begin with an activity a child is already fine with and then build on that in tiny increments. Sam's story at the end of this chapter illustrates this.

From a psychological perspective, it is important to understand that if we are frightened of a certain experience, we will avoid it. Every time we avoid it, it reinforces that anxiety response. If we confront our fear and end up feeling distressed, this also reinforces the anxiety response. The key is to confront feared stimuli in a very gentle, manageable way, so that we have the experience of a small amount of manageable anxiety followed by the experience of not being distressed and seeing that nothing catastrophic happened.

Frequency

Rather than putting a lot of effort into dramatic and exciting opportunities for sensory play, look for small, frequent opportunities, embedded in the other activities that are going on. Maybe you are sowing seeds with the children – give them the opportunity to bury their hands in the soil. Maybe you are clearing away from an art activity – allow children to cover their hands in paint and make a few hand prints before you wash everything up.

SAM'S STORY

Sam was a three-year-old who would only eat dry foods. He had been attending pre-school for a few months now and had settled well, except that he was very wary about getting his hands dirty or sticky and took a long time to warm to new activities and people. His key worker, Rebekah, wanted to help him get used to different textures. She got some jelly, put it in a tub and invited him to see how it felt. Sam didn't want to try this, but stuck his finger in after a bit of persuasion and then became extremely upset.

Rebekah's line manager, Adam, who was a very experienced early years practitioner, reviewed what had happened with Rebekah. He suggested that she had perhaps gone too far, too fast, with Sam. He thought it could be a good idea to get Sam painting with a paintbrush, and then work towards finger painting. When he was comfortable with this, Rebekah could see if he could manage using food items to finger paint, like some strawberry sauce. Once he was comfortable with a little sauce on a fingertip, he could perhaps see how it felt decorating a jelly. Finally, he could try the activity where he played with the jelly in a tub.

Rebekah followed Adam's advice – it took several weeks with lots of very gentle exposures which were increasingly challenging, until Sam did some baking one day and spontaneously put mixture all over his hands, with no sign of discomfort. He wasn't able to eat foods with sauces yet but, if his confidence and tolerance of different textures continued to improve, Adam and Rebekah hoped it wouldn't be too long before his eating confidence grew too.

Food play is great for all children, whether they experience challenges like sensory sensitivity and picky eating, or not. Use play in your setting to help children learn about mealtime behaviour, to increase their familiarity with a wide variety of foods and to help build curiosity and positive associations in relation to food.

Chapter 28

HELPING CHILDREN ENGAGE WITH THEIR FOOD

Researchers looking at the amount of fruit and vegetables eaten by three- and four-year-olds attending eight nurseries in Yorkshire found that these children's consumption was falling very short of the recommended 'five a day'. They suggested that children must be: 'exposed to a variety of fruit and vegetables in order to increase both awareness and liking, and in turn to increase consumption'.[1] This fits with what we know about the importance of exposure, discussed earlier in the book.

To increase children's awareness and liking of foods that may be unfamiliar, we need to tap into that infectious enthusiasm that they have in copious supply. You will know that the route to getting young children excited about something is not to impart information 'at them' but to pique their interest and excitement; to engage them. Children are naturally very curious about the world around them and there is lots we can do to make them inquisitive and excited about the food we eat. If we can provide lots of opportunities to get children connected to and engaged with their food, their awareness will increase automatically. Let's look at a few ways we can engage children with their food.

COOKING

Cooking with children is such a lovely thing to do, and is a regular activity in many settings. Not only does it give children lots of exposure to sensory stimuli, it also teaches them about what our food is made of, and they are able to feel more connected to it. Cake is no longer just cake – it becomes flour, eggs, sugar and butter... The magic, transformational quality of cooking makes it so appealing to children, not to mention the fun of eating the results of their hard work.

When you plan cooking or food preparation activities, try to use them as an opportunity to introduce new foods. You could make a courgette cake rather than plain fairy cakes, for example. Or you could help the children create their own salads from a selection of ingredients, or decorate their own pizzas. It is great to provide multiple exposures to a new food over time, by taking a different recipe each week that uses the same ingredient.

GARDENING

If your setting has the space, the children will love growing their own fruit and vegetables. If they sow a fast-growing seed like a radish, this will help them make the connection between what we eat and our planet. They will see that their seedlings need water, sunshine and nutrients in order to survive, and will begin to appreciate the journey their food makes before it gets to their plate. This is also a very effective analogy for illustrating how we too, need nutrients, water and exercise to survive and thrive.

You can grow plants like runner beans in a planter, with very little space. Children will really enjoy seeing a bean plant grow – and they will get an exposure to beans every time they go out to water it or check on the progress of the pods. There are so many opportunities for cross-curricular learning here too; they can measure their beans or think about Jack and his beanstalk! Like cooking, gardening can foster some fantastic positive associations with food. If a child feels proud of themselves for growing something that they and their peers can eat, all these positive emotions will be associated with that food.

It is essential to see cooking and gardening as exposure activities in and of themselves. If you are working with a child who is a picky eater and may be resistant to actually tasting the food they have helped cook or grow, that's fine. They have already benefited hugely, simply by engaging with a new or disliked food in a positive way. Trying to persuade them to try some if they are unwilling can undo all those fantastic positive associations that were built up while they had fun with the activity. Seeing the goal as eating the food is to look at the activity from the perspective of an adult. We cook something, we eat it. It's the natural conclusion to our efforts. However, for a child, engaging in the process is equally (if not more) important.

VISITS

Taking children on trips to learn more about where our food comes from is a brilliant way of helping them feel connected to their food. Take them to a petting farm where they can watch a cow being milked and maybe collect some eggs from the hens. Take them to a greengrocer's shop or a market stall to learn about all the different vegetables they will find there.

Educational trips don't need to be expensive or dramatic; a visit to the fruit and vegetable section of your local supermarket could provide a great basis for an outing! It is easy to fit visits thematically into your planning so that the children can get lots out of them, while also engaging with their food.

If your setting is in an urban area, there may still be opportunities to visit city farms and farmer's markets. In fact, towns and cities often present more opportunities for children to learn about different fruits and vegetables than rural areas. This is especially true where there is a high level of ethnic diversity. Children can learn about fruit and vegetables from other cultures and can experience different cuisines and cultural celebrations.

ART

We looked at the power of using food in play in the previous chapter – it is such a valuable way of helping children develop a positive relationship with food. Enabling children to explore new foods in a playful way is a very simple route towards raising awareness and giving them exposures to new foods. Harness their creativity – for example, they could make pasta and pulse art, assuming this was appropriate to their age and stage. Of course, when working with real food, it is essential that you have appropriate supervision in place.

THINKING ABOUT WASTE

Some people are uncomfortable with the waste that is often part and parcel of creative or exploratory activities with food. This is a valid sentiment; we ought not to be complacent about how privileged we are to have enough to eat, unlike many people in other countries and indeed in the UK.

The Trussell Trust releases data on the use of UK foodbanks twice a year.[2] The latest figures show that in one year (to March 2017), the Trussell Trust's foodbank network distributed over a million three-day emergency food supplies to people in need. Although they are the biggest network, the Trussell Trust are not the only organisation running food banks, so the overall figure will be even higher. Food poverty in Great Britain is a huge issue.

I believe that it's important to get the balance right between the acknowledgement of food poverty and the need for children to be exposed to a wide variety of foods. Accepting that some waste is inevitable does not mean that food needs to be treated in a disrespectful way. This balance will be something every setting will have to think through for themselves. My message is that giving children plenty of exposures to a wide variety of foods is essential but this needs to be managed in a manner that is respectful and aware.

JOYFUL EATING

When I talk about joyful eating, I am thinking about what we model when we eat. In Chapter 19, we looked at the significance of the messages we unconsciously send when we interact with or talk about food. Joyful eating is simply about us engaging with our food with joy and enthusiasm, not it a false way, but with authenticity. Genuine enthusiasm is infectious!

This is especially powerful if you eat the same food as the children at your setting, but if you bring in your own food, it is important too. Do you look forward to your food? Are you excited about it? Do you talk about where it comes from? We are not all foodies and for some, food is just fuel. But if everyone spends a bit more time and care preparing their food and takes a bit more joy in eating it, this will have an impact on your eating environment in general and on the children in your care.

● ● ● ● ● SECTION 9 ●

A CLOSER LOOK AT PICKY EATING

In this section, we will think about how to define and conceptualise picky eating. An important part of this process involves understanding whether it is developmentally normal and, if so, what this means for practice. We will be exploring what causes picky eating and I will emphasise the importance of trying to understand what is behind a child's eating behaviours, when thinking about the support they need. I will share some core principles to use when working with picky eaters as well as some strategies which can help children learn to enjoy a more varied diet.

PICKY EATING
Is there really a problem?

In this chapter, we'll be examining the term 'picky eating'. How can we define it and is it a useful label? We'll also be looking at whether picky eating should be seen as a problem or simply as a developmentally normal phase.

WHAT IS PICKY EATING?

If I am honest, I dislike the term 'picky eating'. I think that it has negative connotations and puts blame on the child. It also implies choice. Most of the 'picky eaters' I have worked with genuinely wished they could eat a broader range of foods and were not simply being 'choosy', 'finicky' or 'fussy'.

You may be wondering why I choose to use it when I feel this way. Well, it is widely used in the academic literature and it is also extensively used online and in popular parenting articles. Importantly, it is the phrase most parents use. In my clinical work, I talk about 'limited' or 'anxious' eaters but these terms are not commonly used. Some people use 'selective eaters' but selective eating disorder is sometimes employed as a diagnostic label (see Chapter 33) and I prefer to avoid these clinical associations. For now, it seems 'picky eating' is a term we are stuck with.

There is a lack of a clear consensus on a definition of picky eating amongst researchers.[1,2] However, I use it to refer to eating behaviours characterised by:

- acceptance of a limited range of foods
- strong food preferences
- food neophobia (a fear of new or unfamiliar foods).

When we consider picky eating, we usually think about the acceptance of a limited range of foods and food rejection. However, strong food preferences are the other side of the same coin. If a child only accepts a limited range of foods and is wary of unfamiliar foods, it follows that they will cling with force to the foods that they do accept. These accepted foods are often referred to by feeding professionals as 'safe foods'; I like this term as it encapsulates some of the anxiety experienced by very picky eaters.

HOW COMMON IS PICKY EATING?

Picky eating is very common, although it is hard to put a precise figure on it. A recent UK review of the literature found[3] that the statistics varied across studies and across countries. The findings ranged from less than 6 per cent in Holland (looking at Dutch four-year-olds) to 50 per cent of two-year-olds in the USA. A recent Portuguese study[4] carried out after this review was published, found that 25 per cent of children aged between 18 months and five years were picky eaters. Another study[5] refers to prevalence of between 14 and 50 per cent.

Arriving at an accurate figure is problematic because of the lack of a clear definition of picky eating, described above, coupled with variations in the assessment methods used. However, I think it would be a fair to say that approximately one quarter of toddlers and pre-schoolers may be picky eaters. It could be argued that if it is such a common phenomenon, perhaps picky eating is a normal stage children go through, and should not be seen as problem at all. Let's look at this a little more closely.

IS PICKY EATING JUST A PHASE?

Health professionals often regard picky eating as a phase which will pass with time, although parents experience it very differently, often finding it very worrying and then feeling frustrated when their concerns are dismissed when they seek help.[6] Before we think about whether this is a useful mindset, let's explore whether it really is 'just a phase'.

Research shows that most children do simply grow out of picky eating. Dutch researchers carried out a study[7] which was part of the 'Generation R' project: research following several thousand children over many years. Picky eating was assessed when the children were 18 months, then three years and finally, six years old. Data was provided for just over 4000 children at each of these stages of their development. The scale of this study and the fact that it was carried out over a long period of time make the results especially noteworthy. This research found that the highest rate of picky eating was at three years of age (27.6%) and the lowest at six years of age (13.2%). Nearly two thirds of the children who were picky at three, were no longer picky aged six:

> This suggests that picky eating in preschool children is a transient behavior which may be seen as part of normal development.[8]

However, clearly that final third of children were still picky aged six, and parents of picky eaters of all ages find it to be a very real source of stress and concern. My feeling is that while it may be useful from a professional perspective to be aware that most children grow out of picky eating – and it can be reassuring for parents to know this too – this should not form a basis for dismissing it.

For those children who will grow out of picky eating, we can help them through it, via the use of informed and competent practice. This will hopefully minimise the stress they experience. When faced with a three-year-old who is a picky eater, we don't yet know which group that child will fall into; if we ignore their negative relationship with food and hope that they will simply move out of that phase, we have a one in three chance of being disappointed!

Ultimately, if there is any way we can work to help a child access a varied, healthy diet, we should do that. I recommend treating the view that picky eating is a phase with sensitivity and caution. In Chapter 24, we looked at how parents can feel judged (and can also judge themselves) in relation to their child's eating. We can use the data on picky eating to help them understand that what they are experiencing is a standard part of childhood for many children. We can explain that their child may naturally outgrow these behaviours but that we hear their concern and there are things they can do to make things better. Seeing a behaviour as potentially temporary does not have to equate to dismissing it.

JUST HOW BAD IS IT?

I think it is useful to make a distinction between extreme picky eating and more 'common or garden' picky eating. There is a huge array of food rejection behaviours that you will come across in your practice, ranging from mild, to behaviours that would constitute a disorder (see Chapter 33). Dr Kay Toomey is an internationally renowned American Pediatric Psychologist who developed the SOS approach to assessing and treating children with feeding problems. She proposes a distinction between picky eaters and 'problem feeders' who reject entire texture categories and accept 20 foods or fewer.[9] Other experts describe a picky eater (as opposed to a 'problem eater') as a child who accepts at least 30 foods.[10] Whatever number we put on it, it is useful to be aware that there is a difference between a normally picky child and a child with more profound issues.

To conclude, the question about whether picky eating is normal is a complex one. The answer is that it is a natural stage of development which many children go through. In most cases children grow out of it. In some cases, they don't. We shouldn't dismiss it as 'just a phase' because there are many things we can do to support the acceptance of a varied diet. If we are not dismissing it, should we see it as 'a problem'? US dietitian and family nutrition expert Maryann Jacobsen, suggests not:

> Once you stop viewing picky eating as a problem, you will see you have some work to do in teaching your child about food and guiding her in the right direction. Food is no different from other learned skills, like reading and writing.[11]

Let's embrace a learning model of eating – every child is at a different point on their journey towards a varied diet. We can understand picky behaviours as developmentally normal, while also being mindful that for many parents they are a genuine source of stress, and for a small minority of children, their eating constitutes a significant problem and will have an enormous impact on their daily lives.

- Whether a child is not remotely picky, is slightly picky or has a high level of eating issues, as a practitioner you can be supportive of all of these children by fostering good feeding practices in your setting and helping children learn to enjoy a varied diet.

————————————————

Chapter 30

WHAT IS BEHIND PICKY EATING?

In the previous chapter, we explored whether picky eating was a developmentally normal phase. We concluded that it is, in that many children become picky in toddlerhood and have grown out of it by the time they are six years old. We also considered why – despite this – it can be unhelpful to characterise picky eating as 'just a phase', because this can result in a dismissive rather than constructive attitude.

There are two main arguments for why so many children may become picky. The first is an evolutionary argument,[1] whereby scientists look at behaviours in terms of the survival of the human race. They speculate that if children avoid eating things that are unfamiliar, this will reduce the risk of them ingesting something toxic. This makes a lot of sense when we think about at what age picky eating usually begins; it seems to coincide with children gaining in mobility and independence. Perhaps, at the very point that children are learning to walk and can wander off by themselves to pick a poisonous berry, a protective mechanism kicks in, making them wary of anything that they don't recognise as a familiar food.

It is also worth noting that children's taste buds are not like ours; not only do children taste things more intensely than adults, they also have a preference for sweet, salty and sometimes sour foods, avoiding bitter tastes.[2] It has been suggested that this aversion to bitterness could also be a mechanism to protect young children from poisonous substances.

Another argument concerning the emergence of picky eating in toddlerhood is centred around where children are developmentally.

As anyone who has worked with toddlers will know, between 12 and 24 months children are making some rapid developmental shifts, moving from being dependant babies to increasingly independent children. This is not always an easy transition and is characterised by powerful emotions which toddlers are only just learning about managing. Let's consider the following aspects of this developmental stage[3] in relation to eating and good practice:

INCREASING LEVELS OF INDEPENDENCE

Toddlers are beginning to learn about their own autonomy and they are usually keen to assert themselves. This can manifest itself during mealtimes via an emphatic expression of their preferences. They want the blue cup, the banana which has no brown on it and they want to feed themselves! If we take an excessively controlling approach to these types of behaviours, some toddlers may respond with an even greater need to exert control. On the other hand, if we are too compliant and passive, they may push to see where the limits lie. In both cases, this can manifest as picky eating.

DIFFICULTY BEING DIRECTED BY ADULTS

It is normal for toddlers to challenge adult expectations about their behaviour. They are trying to ascertain where their autonomy ends, and part of this is about testing boundaries. What may look like 'bad' behaviour is often a child trying to find out exactly where the boundaries are – and whether they are genuine – simply because they need this knowledge in order to feel safe.

At mealtimes, as elsewhere, boundaries need to be maintained calmly, kindly and consistently. Food can easily become an arena for boundary testing and the use of controlling feeding practices (see Section 2) exacerbates this. When we are thinking about mealtime boundaries, it is useful to reflect on the distinction between having expectations about mealtime behaviour and having expectations about what children eat (in the context of what has been provided). The former is supportive of a positive relationship with food, the latter is not.

GREATER AWARENESS OF RESTRICTIONS IN RELATION TO BEHAVIOUR

This is part and parcel of developmentally normal boundary testing and autonomy seeking. Toddlers are beginning to get a clear sense of what they can't do! Part of their exploration of this involves pushing against those restrictions. If they feel that they are not allowed to make their own eating decisions, they may unconsciously challenge this by sticking to a limited range of foods.

INCREASING UNDERSTANDING OF OTHERS' DISLIKES AND LIKES

As toddlers learn that other people have certain preferences, they may start to express their own likes and dislikes in relation to others. Preferences can begin to become a part of identity: 'I don't like to eat green things!' This can be emphasised by the language we use around food. If we state that 'Katie doesn't like cabbage' rather than, 'Maybe Katie will like the cabbage next time' or 'Katie is learning to like cabbage' we can inadvertently contribute to food preferences forming part of a child's sense of self.

EMERGING SKILLS OF EMOTIONAL MANAGEMENT

Toddlers are often in the grip of big emotions. They can move from 'everything is great' to 'the world has ended' in 0.3 seconds. Cleaving to the familiar during mealtimes can be a way of managing big feelings, like anxiety or anger. If a toddler is unsure about a new food or is simply feeling the pressure of a social situation, they may limit which foods they will accept as a means of feeling more in control. In other words, picky eating can be a coping strategy. Rather than focusing on a child's eating decisions, support their emotional management skills at mealtimes by giving them better ways of dealing with difficult feelings, like using their words.

WHAT DOES THIS DEVELOPMENTALLY NORMAL PICKY PERIOD MEAN FOR PRACTITIONERS?

All of these hallmarks of toddlerhood can contribute to picky eating because what a child eats is one of the few things that they have a measure of control over. As we saw in Chapter 7, when they limit the range of foods they will eat, or reject foods, this can result in a dramatic reaction from adults. Any reaction – whether positive or negative – can be experienced as a pay-off by young children. It is a perfect storm; toddlers may be naturally inclined to stick with food that is familiar, their eating may be an effective way of testing the extent of their autonomy and their eating decisions may be met with a reaction that is exciting and rewarding for them.

Toddlers also have short attention spans and may simply experiment with food rejection because they are bored. This is especially likely if they are not particularly hungry. We can mitigate this in two ways: by using an appropriate meal and snack structure to optimise appetite and by seeing our mealtime role as being about engaging children socially and creating a positive eating environment. A child who is connected to the people around them and is focused on communicating with others is much less likely to get bored at mealtimes.

We need to recognise that picky eating is (mostly) developmentally normal. We need to maintain clear boundaries in terms of the content and structure of meals (see Chapter 3) and let children make their own eating decisions. As long as we continue to expose children to a varied diet in a positive eating environment, most should move out of this picky phase without too much drama.

MORE COMPLEX CAUSES OF PICKY EATING

It would be wrong to explore the causes of picky eating without acknowledging that for some children, picky eating is not just about normal features of development. In my clinical experience, these are the children who are less likely to grow out of this picky stage and who accept the most limited range of foods. There seem to be four main causes of picky eating besides the developmentally normal phenomena discussed in this chapter so far. These are anxiety, temperament, sensory processing and autism spectrum disorder (ASD). You will find chapters dedicated to sensory processing and ASD in Section 10 of this book.

Children who are sensory sensitive are more likely to be picky eaters, as are anxious children. Research shows that these things are potentially linked; it has been suggested that children who are anxious are more likely to be sensitive to sensory information.[4] Equally, children who are temperamentally cautious are likely to be wary of new or unfamiliar foods.

I see anxiety as the unifying factor across all more extreme manifestations of picky eating. Building on Toomey's classification of problem feeders as distinct from developmentally normal picky eaters, I would suggest a differentiation of anxious picky eaters and non-anxious picky eaters. The latter group is more likely to be responding to controlling feeding practices or an eating environment that is less than ideal.

This is supported by one of the observations made by Anya Bell, the nursery cook I interviewed for the case study at the end of this book. She explained that once the eating environment was right, staff at the setting were able to see who the children with more worrying eating issues were. Children who had been moderately picky before ate much better once optimum feeding practices were in place.

I would suggest that a child can be anxious about eating something disliked or unfamiliar for many reasons. Maybe they are on the autism spectrum and find novelty inherently challenging. Maybe they are cautious by nature, and need things to be familiar before they are comfortable with them. Maybe they have a high level of sensory sensitivity and are overwhelmed by the smell, taste and texture of new foods. If an experience is hard for a child, it follows that they will feel anxious about it and will try to avoid it. We need to empathise with that anxiety. We need to help children feel in control during meals, while giving them many exposures to new and disliked foods so that they will become less scary.

Every child is different and I would never advocate taking a 'one size fits all' approach to picky eating. On the contrary, if you have concerns about picky eating, I recommend trying to get some insights into what is driving that child's eating behaviours. Understanding the root cause of picky eating is at the heart of effective support for children. Sometimes you will have a sense of what is at play, other times you may need to seek additional input from appropriate professionals.

- Chapter 31

CORE PRINCIPLES WHEN WORKING WITH PICKY EATERS

This chapter contains an overview of how to respond to picky eating in a way that will both support children and ensure that eating issues are not exacerbated. This will involve summaries of ideas already expressed elsewhere in this book, because sometimes an accessible reminder of best practice is useful.

FIRST STEPS – IS THERE A REFERRAL TO BE MADE?

If you are concerned about a child in your care because you think that they are not accessing a varied and healthy diet, there are a few questions you need to ask yourself.

Could neglect be an issue?

In other words, does the child have access to appropriate foods (if they are bringing their food in from home)? You will have a clear policy to follow if you suspect neglect.

Is this concern part of a wider picture?

Are you thinking about referring this child for assessment for special educational needs or disability (SEND) or are they having treatment or assessment for any medical problems? It is always important to see the whole child, and picky eating can often be associated with other factors, both physical and developmental.

Have they had a recent weight and growth check by a health professional?

All reception children will be offered a weight and growth review by the school nurse. However, if you are concerned about a child's eating, it is a good idea to suggest to parents that the school nurse checks their weight and growth sooner than this. If parents prefer, they could see their GP or their health visitor. All of these professionals would be in a position to make or suggest an appropriate onward referral, if a child's weight and growth is not on track. This is very important because issues with weight and growth may signal another underlying problem, such as digestive issues or problems swallowing food.

SPEAKING TO PARENTS

Maybe you have noticed that a child is a picky eater and this has not previously been brought to your attention by parents. This is often the case, as parents may feel judged and defensive when it comes to their child's eating behaviours and may not willingly bring the subject up. They may also not see their child's eating as problematic in the first instance.

It would be constructive to arrange a time for you or a colleague to speak with parents about your concerns. At that meeting, it would be useful to get a clear picture of the food environment at home, so that you can better understand the child's needs. It is also useful to get a feel for whether parents perceive picky eating to be a problem and want to work with you to improve their child's eating.

As discussed in Section 7, if a parent doesn't want support, forcing the issue can do more harm than good if it results in a deterioration of your relationship with that parent. However, the child must always be your main priority and if parents refuse to seek appropriate medical support, in some cases this needs to be handled with reference to your child protection policy.

It can be very constructive to normalise and destigmatise picky eating by explaining to parents that it is a common challenge and that you are neither judging nor blaming them. The key message to convey is that a child's relationship with food is something you can work on together. Focus on looking at some consistent practices to use across home and your setting.

PRACTICES TO SHARE

Rather than inundate families with too much information, here are some key tips which will make a huge difference to picky eating.

- Keep to a clear meal and snack structure – avoiding grazing – with at least two hours, and not more than three, between eating opportunities.

- Use Satter's division of responsibility[1] (see Chapter 3) to understand your role in relation to food.

- Eat at a table (without screens or distraction) as much as possible.

- Eat together as a family as much as possible.

- Always include at least one accepted food (safe food) with every meal and snack.

- If a child leaves all or part of what they have been offered, don't provide an alternative (this is fine in the context of the previous tip having been followed, because part of that meal or snack will have included a safe food).

- Provide new foods alongside safe foods, introducing new foods that are as similar to safe foods as possible as well as other, more ambitious, items.

- Rotate and slightly alter safe foods as much as possible, in order to maximise the variety in a child's diet.

- Never encourage children to eat, whether through bribing, reasoning, insisting, bargaining and so on. Leave them to make their own eating decisions.

- Take the focus of meals away from what and how children are eating – instead, talk about everyone's day and try to enjoy each other's company.

- Try hard to make sure mealtimes are relaxed and positive.

Chapter 32

STRATEGIES TO HELP PICKY EATERS

In this chapter, we will be looking at what you can do in your setting to empower picky eaters to move beyond their safe foods and begin to access a varied diet.

PROVIDING A SAFETY NET

A great strategy to use for all children, but especially those who are wary of unfamiliar foods, is to have a small bowl or plate onto which each child can serve themselves items they are not sure about. Some specialists call this a tasting or learning bowl. This approach is much less scary for children than having a new food served directly onto their main plate. It opens up the potential for them to try something without any pressure at all. It is also useful to give children the option to (politely and discretely) spit foods out if they try them and don't like them. That way, they can feel secure in the knowledge that trying a new food is not a commitment to swallowing it. This gives them a valuable safety net.

It is fantastic to show children that if we want to learn to like a new food, we can get more familiar it in lots of different ways, not solely by eating it. We can smell it, handle it, lick it, kiss it…even put it on our tongues before spitting it out. To conceptualise swallowing a mouthful of a new food as the central goal is mistaken. Instead, our goal should be children having positive exposures to new foods. It can take a very long time and many exposures for a child to learn to like something new. Just being interested and smelling it, or perhaps putting it to the lips before replacing it on the plate, would be a baby step in the right direction. Swallowing something in response to pressure and having a negative experience as a result would be two steps back.

BUILDING BLOCKS

The next strategy I want to share is a great way of helping picky eaters expand their repertoire. This may not be applicable for you if you don't have control over what food is served at meal or snack times. However, if you are a childminder or can work with the cook on menu planning, it can be extremely powerful. I call this strategy 'building blocks' because it is about building on the foundations that are already in place. It is a two-phase approach. The first phase is all about helping children get used to small changes in their safe foods, and the second phase is about helping them learn to accept new foods which are just a tiny bit different from their safe foods.

In the first phase, if they are used to apple slices at snack time you could serve grated apple instead. This is essentially the same food but in a different format. When a child accepts small alterations to their safe foods like this, you can increase the amount of variation. For example, if a child eats pasta spirals (fusilli) you could serve the red versions of the same pasta.

If we understand that many children who are picky eaters are limiting the number of foods they will accept in order to feel secure, it makes sense that clinging to the familiar is a really important part of this dynamic. If we can help children learn experientially (rather than through what we tell them) that they can have pasta that is a different shape or colour and nothing catastrophic happens, they can slowly begin to gain in confidence when it comes to trying new and disliked foods.

The American book *Food Chaining*[1] describes a similar method where a path is mapped out from an accepted food to a food which is a target for that child, using small, manageable steps. The key is building on what a child will already accept. Adults and children have different perspectives on what novelty entails. We might serve a child some green beans when they only eat beige food, in the hope that they will be open to trying the beans. What we need to understand is that these beans represent a superhuman leap away from what that child knows and feels safe with. However, if we give a child a new food which is a little different, but also beige and crunchy, this is a much more realistic option.

Empathy is key when working with picky eaters. I sometimes use the (horribly graphic!) metaphor of going to a restaurant and being served a plate with a parsley-garnished rotten octopus on it. We would be horrified and nothing would induce us to try it. This is what it is like for a child who is a very picky eater. The prospect of eating something disliked or unfamiliar is by turns disgusting and terrifying. We need to meet children where they are and work with them to increase their eating repertoire from within the security of their comfort zone.

● ● ● ● ● SECTION 10 ●

SPECIAL CASES

In this section, we will look at some of the more specialist areas in terms of children's eating. I offer an overview of Avoidant Restrictive Food Intake Disorder (ARFID) and touch briefly on the history of classifying extremely limited eating in childhood. I discuss allergies and intolerances with a view to suggesting how to meet children's needs in a psychologically healthy way. There is a chapter dedicated to autism spectrum disorder (ASD) as many autistic children have eating issues, and a chapter about sensory processing. We'll look at oral motor skills because when children have problems with chewing and swallowing, this can have an enormous impact on their relationship with food. Finally, I will talk about the very current issue of childhood obesity.

Chapter 33

AVOIDANT RESTRICTIVE FOOD INTAKE DISORDER

Avoidant Restrictive Food Intake Disorder (ARFID) is a diagnostic label used for certain children whose eating is extremely limited. In this chapter, we are going to cover ARFID because I think it is important for practitioners to know that this clinical diagnosis exists. We will look at the history of this diagnosis and what ARFID entails. Finally, we will touch on the implications for you as a practitioner.

First, a little foray into the world of psychiatry. There are two main diagnostic manuals used by psychiatrists and related professionals. These are the ICD-10,[1] which is produced by the World Health Organization (WHO) and the DSM-5,[2] produced by the American Psychiatric Association (APA). ICD stands for International Classification of Diseases and DSM stands for Diagnostic and Statistical Manual.

These manuals are updated every few years and the ICD-11 is due to come out in 2018. The DSM-5 was published in 2013 and was not without its detractors. Several organisations, including the British Psychological Society (BPS), have been critical of the DSM-5, arguing that it goes too far in terms of medicalising mental disorders, prioritising medication over talking to the patient themselves and drawing on psychological theory.[3]

Whether we agree with current diagnostic practices or not – and diagnosing children is an especially contentious area – this is the system that is used in the NHS today, as well as in America and elsewhere in the world. In the previous version of the DSM (DSM-IV), young children who would now receive a diagnosis of ARFID would have been classified as having 'Feeding Disorders of Infancy and Early Childhood'. This was a vague, catch-all label, limited in terms of the age-span it covered. ARFID, however, has more precise symptomatology and is not limited in terms of age as it also includes adults and older children.[4] ARFID is likely to be included in the ICD-11 when it is published.[5]

There have been several labels attached to extremely limited eating in childhood, such as Selective Eating Disorder (SED) and Food Avoidance Emotional Disorder (FAED). These (and other) disorders were suggested by feeding specialists at Great Ormond Street Hospital who found that the available diagnostic system did not reflect the needs of their patients. Their classification of eating disorders is known as the Great Ormond Street Criteria.[6] American researcher, Irene Chatoor,[7] also proposed a diagnostic category called 'sensory food aversion' to reflect the sensory issues experienced by many very limited eaters.

These conditions or disorders are not included in the current diagnostic manuals and ARFID is intended to cover the symptoms they comprise. However, it is worth knowing as a practitioner that many professionals do still use this terminology and you may well encounter medical professionals talking about SED, for example.

THE SYMPTOMS OF ARFID

It is not my aim to give you a complete overview of how ARFID is diagnosed. As with any clinical diagnosis, this is the remit of an appropriately qualified professional like a clinical psychologist or a psychiatrist. However, these are the key symptoms of ARFID listed in the DSM-5.[8]

A child with ARFID has a problem with eating such as not showing any interest in food, avoiding foods because of their sensory characteristics or fear that something bad will happen if they eat certain foods. They consistently fail to eat enough to meet their requirements for energy and nutrients. At least *one* of the following must also be true:

- They are either not thriving and putting on weight in accordance with expectations for their age, or they are losing weight.

- They have a significant nutritional deficiency.

- They rely on supplements which they take by mouth, or they are fed by a feeding tube.

- There is marked interference with their psychosocial functioning.

- Their eating behaviours cannot better be explained by other factors, like fasting for religious reasons or because they don't have access to enough food.

WHAT DOES THIS MEAN FOR PRACTITIONERS?

A notable feature of ARFID is that a child may meet the diagnostic criteria without being underweight or having a nutritional deficiency.[9] This is because the psychosocial aspect of very limited eating is acknowledged. I think this is extremely important because it recognises just how crippling eating problems can be. If you are working with a child whose eating problems are so extreme that they are having an impact on that child's ability to function socially or access aspects of your provision, this needs to be taken seriously.

It is no longer the case that children's eating problems can be dismissed because they are not under-weight or inadequately nourished. In the past, some doctors would only look at the physical health of a child with very limited eating, missing the psychological and social struggles that child may have been experiencing. Now ARFID has been included in the DSM-5, this should no longer be happening.

ALLERGIES AND INTOLERANCES

Most early years practitioners will have come across children with food allergies and intolerances. A recent review of the research carried out across Europe found that at least one in twenty children has a food allergy or intolerance.[1] In this chapter, we'll be exploring what the difference is between an allergy and intolerance and we'll be thinking about relevant good practice. Some knowledge of the medical aspects involved in this area is important, especially knowing how to recognise anaphylactic shock and how to use an EpiPen. However, this information is beyond the scope of the book.

ALLERGIES

Technically, an allergy is a 'hypersensitivity' reaction triggered by the immune system.[2] Let's look at what this actually means. A hypersensitivity is when a person consistently reacts to a stimulus when most people would not react to the same amount of that stimulus. The second important aspect of this definition is that the reaction is an immune response. In other words, someone can be said to be allergic to something if their body's defence system reacts to it in a way that other people's do not.

The substance causing the allergic reaction is called an 'allergen'. The most common allergens are cow's milk, egg, wheat, soy, peanut, tree nuts, fish and shellfish, with cow's milk and egg allergies being most frequently seen in young children. Research findings vary greatly in terms of what percentage of people have food allergies, ranging from 0.1 per cent to 6 per cent.[3]

It is important to know what an allergy really is because it is a term that is often used casually or incorrectly. If a parent tells you their child has a food allergy, you need to be sure that this is the case and have a clear understanding of the severity of that allergy. According to the European Academy of Allergy and Clinical Immunology (EAACI), best practice in relation to allergies is to have an allergy policy and individual allergy management plans for children with allergies.[4] Allergies can be life threatening and must always be taken very seriously.

FOOD INTOLERANCES

Food intolerances are more common than food allergies, affecting 15 to 20 per cent of the population.[5] Scientists define food intolerances as a range of food-related symptoms with varying causes.[6] They are not an immune reaction and they are not a reaction to something that would be toxic for everybody, like food poisoning is. Food intolerances often cause problems for the digestive system (gastrointestinal problems).[7]

COELIAC DISEASE

Coeliac disease is neither an allergy nor an intolerance, but an autoimmune condition.[8] I have included it because it has similar implications to allergies and intolerances for the children who suffer from it. Coeliac disease manifests itself in different ways in different individuals. It is a reaction to gluten, which is found in wheat, rye and barley. Symptoms of Coeliac disease include diarrhoea, weight loss, bloating and abdominal pain.[9]

SUPPORTING CHILDREN: A BALANCING ACT

Supporting children who can't eat certain foods is a challenge. This is because it involves competing needs. On the one hand, you need to keep children safe and well. On the other hand, you need to help them feel integrated in the group and avoid singling them out as much as possible. Bringing in tension or anxiety is extremely damaging to children's relationship with food. Here are some suggestions about how to get the balance right.

Inform children

Teach all the children in your care what an allergy or intolerance is, in an age-appropriate way. Keep the message upbeat. The book *The BugaBees: Friends with Food Allergies* by Amy Recob (see the Resources section for details) teaches children about how to face food allergies with positivity. Children can be a key part of keeping one another safe – make sure they know what an allergic reaction looks like and to tell an adult straight away if they are worried about a friend.

Be calm about allergies and intolerances

It is understandable that many practitioners feel anxious about allergies and intolerances, especially if they have a child in their care with a severe allergy. You need to be clear about how to make sure they are never exposed to allergens, while being confident that you have sufficient training and knowledge to know what to do if a child did have a reaction. If you are not confident about this, all the children will pick up on your anxiety when you talk about allergies.

Avoid making children feel different

Years ago, before I started working in feeding, my friend brought her daughter with her when she came to my house for a coffee. This little girl had an egg allergy and so I made an egg-free cake for us all. I was so concerned to get it right for my friend's daughter, and was mindful that she often missed out. As soon as they arrived, I showed her the cake, told her it was safe for her and generally made a bit of a song and dance about it. My friend, who is Scandinavian and very direct, quietly took me aside and said she was grateful that I'd been so thoughtful, but she preferred it if people could be a bit more low-key about her daughter's allergy as the attention and focus unnerved her. I learned a valuable lesson that day. I had made the little girl feel different because I was trying so hard to include her!

Try to be relaxed and discrete when you explain to a child with allergies or intolerances which food is safe for them. If you can be matter-of-fact, they can feel calm and accepted. If you are alarmist and dramatic, they will feel alarmed too. I have also worked with families where children have been used to getting a lot of attention via their allergies. This can quickly turn in to something dysfunctional. We need to strive for positive and relaxed mealtimes, while keeping children safe.

AUTISM SPECTRUM DISORDER

A note on terminology: The National Autistic Society recently carried out some research[1] into which terms autistic people favoured when describing themselves. Their study found that, while there is still some debate, most autistic people preferred the 'disability-first' approach, and favoured 'autistic person' over 'person with autism'. They also liked the phrase 'on the autism spectrum'. In line with these findings, this is the terminology I have chosen to use.

In the UK, 1.7 per cent of children are reported to have autism spectrum disorder (ASD). As implied by the name, it is a spectrum; some children may be very high functioning, and others may have extremely complex needs. An issue for early years is that ASD is often not diagnosed until a child is older, although this is improving over time. A review found that the average age for diagnosis was between 38 and 120 months.[2] This implies that some children in your care may ultimately receive a diagnosis, but perhaps not until after they have left your setting. This can be challenging for practitioners, as children do not always have access to the specialist support they need.

WHY IS EATING ESPECIALLY HARD FOR AUTISTIC CHILDREN?

Generalisation is a risky business because each autistic child must be seen as an individual with differing needs and strengths. However, research shows that approximately 80 per cent of young autistic children are picky eaters and 95 per cent are resistant to trying new foods.[3] If you are working with an autistic child, this is something you need to be aware of. While good practice around food applies to all children, neurotypical or not, it is very helpful to understand autistic children's eating issues through the lens of their autism. I'm going to explore some of the factors that make food so tricky for so many autistic children, coupled with some thoughts on how you can help.

A need for routine

Many autistic children find change very difficult. They cling to routine and find comfort in things being predictable and repetitive. Earlier in this book, we looked at the importance of helping children get used to a varied diet and to expect the unexpected. This is really, really hard for an autistic child. Their food routines are often very important to them and any deviation from them can be extremely stressful. It is easy to see how an autistic child can end up with a very limited diet – for them, having the same few foods on rotation is reassuring, just as being served unfamiliar or different foods is potentially frightening and unsettling.

We need to recognise and respect an autistic child's need for routine. However, we also need to help them learn to tolerate new foods in order to expand their eating repertoire and support positive health outcomes. The way to do this is slowly. If a child always has brown toast with butter for breakfast, begin by serving the same toast with a different brand of butter. Then the following week, cut the bread into triangles instead of squares. These tiny changes may not feel useful or important, but they are a route to helping children learn to handle change in a very gentle way. The 'building block' strategy in Chapter 32 uses this approach.

Difficulty expressing responses to food

Verbal and non-verbal communication challenges are a hallmark of ASD. Many autistic children lack language skills and often struggle to express themselves. This can increase stress at mealtimes. If a child is not able to explain how they are experiencing their food and what is tricky about it, this makes it harder for adults to help them. Increased levels of frustration and anxiety can lead to mealtime meltdowns.

If appropriate for a child's abilities, you can help them learn to express feelings about their food by practising away from mealtimes.

Take something they are comfortable with eating and, together, work at describing how you both experience it. Use simple statements like 'this apple is crunchy'; 'I like the sweet taste.'

Behavioural rigidity

Strong preferences are part and parcel of the behavioural rigidity often associated with autism. As we saw in Chapter 29, strong food preferences are also a defining feature of picky eating. An autistic child may cling to their preferred foods with force. Rather than getting into a battle of wills, which will both distress the child and have a negative impact on their relationship with food, introduce new foods alongside old favourites. Try to pick new foods that are similar to their favourites, too.

Socialisation

Scientists[4] exploring autistic children's eating have suggested that difficulty with social interaction can make eating with others especially hard for children on the autism spectrum. I have certainly seen this in my clinical work.

Fine motor skills

Some autistic children may find it hard to use cutlery and may have difficulty mastering and coordinating the fine motor skills required for eating. This can add another level of stress to mealtimes. Adapted cutlery can be a big help in this respect.

Sensory processing issues

There has been an increasing body of research in recent years, looking at autistic children's eating behaviours in the light of sensory sensitivity.[1] Food is extremely stimulating from a sensory perspective. Every autistic child will have different responses to sense data. One child may find smells extremely hard to tolerate whereas another may be visually hypersensitive and find a plate of colourful foods overwhelming. Some children are sensory-seeking and may gravitate towards foods that give them a certain sensory experience.

If a child in your care has had a sensory assessment, you will be much better placed to have an idea of exactly where their difficulties lie. To support them, make sure you set them up to succeed by ensuring that they are not coming to the table overstimulated. A calm activity in the half hour before a meal is a great way of doing this. You can also use physical activities or weighted blankets to help a child who struggles with their vestibular and proprioceptive senses. In the next chapter we will be exploring sensory processing in more depth.

THE EATING ENVIRONMENT

In Chapter 17, we looked at how to optimise the eating environment from a sensory perspective. This is especially important for an autistic child. Based on your knowledge of their particular challenges, try to make the eating environment as close to ideal for them as possible. This may mean finding somewhere quiet for them to eat, away from a crowded, noisy and potentially smelly dining room. Maybe it means dimming the lights slightly or putting on some calming music. You know the children in your care. Work with their parents and any other professionals supporting them, to think through what their specific needs may be in relation to the eating environment.

SENSORY PROCESSING

The term 'sensory integration' was first used by A. Jean Ayres in the 1960s.[1] It is used to describe what our brain does with the data it receives from our senses:

> Sensations flow into our brain like streams flowing into a lake. Countless bits of sensory information enter our brain at every moment, not only from our eyes and ears but from every place in our body.[2]

When the brain integrates this data effectively, these sensations are translated into perceptions. Ayres and Robbins use the analogy of peeling an orange to illustrate how this works:

> All the sensations from the orange, and all the sensations from your fingers and hands somehow come together in one place in your brain, and this integration enables your brain to experience the orange as whole, and to use your hands and fingers together to peel the orange.[3]

We have many senses – not just sight, smell, hearing and touch. For example, we have senses that help us locate our bodies in space and enable us to balance. It is beyond the remit of this book to explore sensory processing in a lot of detail, but you will find some suggested reading in the Resources section. In this chapter, we will look briefly at Sensory Processing Disorder (SPD) and at how sensory processing problems can have an impact on eating.

SPD

SPD is a diagnostic label given to some children who find it hard to integrate sense data. However, it is important to know that the influential American Academy of Pediatrics (AAP) recommended in 2012 that SPD should not generally be used as a diagnosis. There is insufficient evidence that it is a 'stand-alone' disorder. In their policy statement, the AAP wrote:

> Because there is no universally accepted framework for diagnosis, sensory processing disorder generally should not be diagnosed. Other developmental and behavioral disorders must always be considered, and a thorough evaluation should be completed. Difficulty tolerating or processing sensory information is a characteristic that may be seen in many developmental behavioral disorders, including autism spectrum disorders, attention-deficit/hyperactivity disorder, developmental coordination disorders, and childhood anxiety disorders.[4]

Furthermore, SPD has not been included in the DSM-5, which we looked at in Chapter 33.

It is important to note that the AAP are not saying SPD does not exist, just that insufficient research has been done to show that it is a valid classification or to reach a consensus about a definition. The implication is that sensory processing issues are usually part of another disorder, like ASD.

From the point of view of a practitioner concerned about a child's eating, what you need to know is that sensory processing difficulties are a very real phenomenon and they can have a huge impact on a child's relationship with food. This is especially true for autistic children, up to 90 per cent of whom have sensory processing problems.[5]

Sensory processing has been linked to eating challenges in neurotypical children too. Interestingly, researchers have found that it seems to be the senses of touch, smell and taste rather than sound or sight which are relevant when it comes to food rejection.[6] However, if a child is experiencing 'sensory overload' I would expect that being in a noisy and visually stimulating environment will not help!

These are some of the reasons researchers suggested for sensory sensitive children being picky eaters:

- They are able to spot tiny changes in foods.

- They find things that are not all the same (like fruit and vegetables) especially difficult.

- They are likely to be wary of new foods.[7]

As discussed in Chapter 30, anxiety also has a role to play, with sensory sensitivity, picky eating and anxiety seemingly being connected.

IMPLICATIONS FOR PRACTICE

Many children who are very picky eaters have difficulties with texture, taste and smell when it comes to eating. If we understand that they could be finding it hard to process the sense data coming from their food, we can be compassionate and supportive. It might seem easy to us to eat a piece of pasta or chicken, but for a child who finds those textures or smells difficult, it can be overwhelming.

In Chapter 17, we looked at how to create a low-stimulation eating environment which is supportive of children with sensory processing issues. If you are working with a child with a high level of sensory sensitivity, you can also help by preparing them for meals. They will have been bombarded with sensory stimuli throughout their day. Sitting down to a meal could simply be too much for them. If you have the capacity, spend some one-on-one time with the child before they eat. Perhaps you could do some physical activities, like running around or using outdoor play equipment. Perhaps you could do something quiet, like reading a story-book together; whatever works well for that child.

You can support children with sensory processing issues with the building block approach (Chapter 32) because it will enable them to move gently from the textures, tastes and smells they can handle, to new and different foods.

Although it can be very tempting to use controlling feeding practices and try to persuade a child to eat something that they are worried about, in fact this will make them more anxious and more resistant to trying that food in the long run. Focus on helping them relax and giving them appropriate control.

As always, if you have a concern that a child in your care is having an unusual or extreme reaction to sensory stimuli, make sure you make an appropriate referral or share your observations with your manager or the SENCO. Sensory processing problems will rarely manifest solely in relation to food and it could be part of a wider picture in terms of that child's support needs.

———————————————————

Chapter 37

ORAL MOTOR SKILLS

Oral motor problems are a specialist area requiring assessment by an appropriately trained and qualified speech therapist, often called speech and language therapists (SaLTs) in the UK. The purpose of this chapter is not to equip you with expertise in this area, but to raise awareness about the kind of challenges some children face. It will also assist you if you are considering referring a child for evaluation by the SaLT.

It is a common misconception that SaLTs only deal with speech and language problems. While this is a very important aspect of their role, they are often also extremely knowledgeable when it comes to feeding issues. This is because eating has an important physical component and some children may have problems with eating that are connected to their oral motor development.

When we break it down, eating is a very complex process involving many coordinated movements. For example, we move food from one side of the mouth to the other with our tongues, simultaneously using our jaws to chew. Oral motor skills are all of the things we do with our lips, mouth, hard and soft palates tongue, jaw and teeth. In relation to eating, this can be boiled down to the skills of chewing and swallowing, although digestive tract issues may also influence what happens orally. Problems with any aspect of chewing or swallowing can make eating extremely challenging for a child.

Oral motor skills are built gradually over time. They 'represent a sequential progression of increasingly complex movement patterns'.[1] Sometimes children fail to progress from one stage to the next. For example, a child may not move from pureed foods to the acceptance of solids and different textures. If a child is not reaching developmental milestones in relation to eating skills, this needs further investigation.

SOME ORAL MOTOR PROBLEMS YOU MAY COME ACROSS

Dysphagia

Dysphagia is the medical term for swallowing problems. Children with swallowing problems may cough when eating, and may be at a greater risk of choking.

Aspiration

This is when children actually breathe in particles of food and drink. In other words, some of their food or drink goes down their airway rather than their oesophagus.

Tongue problems

Some children may have problems with tongue lateralisation or may have tongue tie. Tongue lateralisation is our ability to move our tongue from side to side. Some children are not able to do this effectively and it can make eating really difficult. Tongue tie is when the bit of tissue connecting the tongue to the base of the mouth (the frenulum) is too short. A child with untreated tongue tie may not be able to stick their tongue out or move their tongue normally.

Saliva

Poor saliva control, which may manifest as dribbling, can be a sign of low jaw tone. If you notice that a child is often drooling, don't ignore this.

Reflux

Although this is technically a problem concerning the digestive tract rather than an oral motor issue, I have included it because it can result in a child gagging, vomiting or coughing while eating. It is the kind of thing a SaLT with feeding expertise would be able to pick up on.

SOME THINGS TO LOOK OUT FOR

In her book for parents,[2] highly respected US speech pathologist, Krisi Brackett (founder of the excellent online resource 'Pediatric Feeding News', see the Resources section), describes some of the signs that a child may have chewing or swallowing problems. These include:

- sucking rather than chewing food
- keeping food in their cheek rather than swallowing it ('pocketing')
- gagging while eating
- vomiting while eating
- coughing while eating
- eyes tearing while eating or drinking
- complaining that food is getting stuck in their throat.

This is by no means an exhaustive list of behaviours which should prompt a referral. Anything you notice that strikes you as unusual when observing a child eating, drinking or speaking, is worth taking note of. Equally, some of these behaviours may not always be symptomatic of an oral motor problem. For example, children may gag due to sensory sensitivity. Eating is a complex business; problems with chewing or swallowing can contribute to behavioural issues in relation to food, as children try to avoid an experience which is tricky or painful for them.

ORAL MOTOR PROBLEMS AND SEND

Children with certain disabilities and special needs (such as Down's syndrome and cerebral palsy) are more likely to have oral motor problems. This ought to be considered as part of their Education, Health and Care (EHC) needs assessment, so make sure you pass on anything you have noticed in relation to that child's eating or drinking, however insignificant it may seem.

WHEN TO REFER

If in doubt, refer. It is always best to seek the advice and input of the SaLT if you have any concerns about a child's chewing or swallowing. As a practitioner, your role is to be observant and tuned in to the children in your care. It is also essential to see the whole child. For example, problems with speech and problems with eating could be connected – the presence of one should make you extra alert to the possibility of the other. It is always a good idea to consider a referral if you have any concerns, if only to rule out oral motor problems.

OBESITY

Obesity rates in the UK are on the rise. We hear this via the media all the time, but what do the statistics say? Well, in England in 1993, 15 per cent of adults were obese. In 2014, the figure was 26 per cent. In that same year, more than one in five reception children was obese.[1] Not only does obesity increase a person's chances of having many common cancers, it is also connected with a range of health and social difficulties, including diseases like type two diabetes, reflux, high blood pressure and sleep apnoea.[2] Research with American adults shows that obesity dramatically reduces life expectancy.[3] It is also important to be aware that poverty is a significant factor when it comes to childhood obesity, with children from the poorest income groups having double the likelihood of being obese than their most well-off counterparts.[4]

The UK government has recently compiled an action plan to tackle childhood obesity.[5] There is an emphasis on reducing sugar in children's diet and on increasing physical activity. However, the plan has been criticised by people like Jamie Oliver[6] for not going far enough. David Buck (Senior Fellow, Public Health and Inequalities) of the King's Fund think tank concludes his critique of the plan by asking: 'where is the delivery plan for a cross-society, cross-government approach to childhood obesity? A bold and brave strategy? Not in those 13 pages.'[7]

What children eat and how much physical activity they have are clearly integral to tackling childhood obesity. Much is said about these by the government, for example through the Change4Life[8] programme. My interest is in the psychological and emotional aspects of childhood eating behaviours and I feel that this also needs to be a prime area of focus when we think about childhood obesity.

There have been some steps in the right direction, like work carried out by the charity HENRY,[9] which offers training that addresses family relationships, behaviour and parenting skills as well as lifestyle. Equally, the legacy left by the Children's Food Trust includes significant progress in terms of how we view children's health and diet. However, my concern is that, as a society, we are not necessarily seeing the whole picture painted by the research evidence.

RESTRICTION

We live in a 'diet' culture, which is all about restriction. We need to be very wary of translating this adult take on weight into a practice of restricting children, which research has shown can be problematic. Restriction is a kind of controlling feeding practice (see Section 2) where an adult imposes limits on a child's eating. Covert restriction is where adults restrict what children eat without their knowledge. Overt restriction, which is very unhelpful, is where adults tell children that they can't have something that is in front of them, or to stop eating – that they have had enough.

The University of Loughborough's excellent Child Feeding Guide website explains:

> There are two types of restriction: **Covert Restriction** refers to restriction that the child cannot see and that they are not aware of. For example, not having unhealthy snack foods in the house or not walking home past the chip shop.
>
> **Overt Restriction** refers to restriction that the child can see and that they are aware of. For example, keeping crisps in the kitchen cupboard, but not allowing your child to eat any, or drinking sugary drinks in front of your child, but not allowing them to have a taste.
>
> Covert restriction is believed to be the most effective way to restrict a child's access to unhealthy foods and drinks, without causing a contrary increase in their desire for such foods.[10]

What is the problem with overt restriction? As well as making unhealthy foods more desirable, it also impedes self-regulation, and children who have lower levels of self-regulation are at a greater risk of obesity.[11] Restricting a child's eating isn't the same as only providing appropriate food in an appropriate structure. It's about trying to impose control on a child's eating decisions, in relation to the food you have made available or visible to them.

It is clear that overt restriction is a way of externally driving children's eating, rather than helping them tune into and respond to their body's cues in the context of the provision of a healthy diet. Academics have known for a long time that excessive overt restriction contributes to weight gain.[12] However, this message does not seem to be getting through in terms of policy. We need to support families in providing nutritious food and enable children to eat in response to their internal signals.

RESPONDING TO CHILDHOOD OBESITY

Here are some thoughts on what the early years sector can do in response to childhood obesity, besides following guidelines on nutrition and promoting an active lifestyle and physical activity:

- provide great quality, fresh food

- help children learn to self-regulate through best practice in relation to feeding

- teach cooking skills and get families enthusiastic about preparing good food from scratch

- help children engage with and get excited about a varied, nutritious diet

- share the message that structured eating, rather than grazing, is supportive of children's health.

It is important that children are not shamed for their bodies – that we understand that people come in a wide range of shapes and sizes. Our goal for our children should be that they can become their healthiest selves and develop positive lifelong habits in relation to how and what they eat.

A CASE STUDY

So far, we have considered what best practice looks like and how you can support children's relationship with food in your setting, in a variety of ways. In this final section, I'd like to share a case study which illustrates how one setting adopted the kinds of evidence-based feeding practices described in this book. It is so useful to learn from other people's experiences and I'm very grateful to Anya Bell, of Nurture Early Learning in New Zealand, for telling me about her journey and allowing me to write about it here, for the benefit of other practitioners.

NURTURE EARLY LEARNING, NEW ZEALAND

Anya Bell is a very experienced cook. She has a background as a professional chef, including training at a high-end hotel in Scotland and a spell working as a chef on private yachts! Her passion is training childcare professionals in facilitating a supportive mealtime environment. Drawing on Satter's division of responsibility and an understanding of the importance of trust in the feeding relationship, Anya helps staff create pressure-free meal and snack times, using family-style serving.

As well as her qualifications in food preparation, Anya is well versed in feeding theory and has undertaken training from the University of Idaho on evidence-based best practice in relation to feeding young children in group settings. Her thorough understanding of cutting-edge thinking, coupled with years of experience as a nursery cook, has put her in the perfect position to spread the word about best practice.

Anya works for Nurture Early Learning, a group of childcare centres (nurseries) in New Zealand. There is an emphasis on real food, cooked from scratch. It sounds idyllic:

> The nutrition programme utilises whole, unprocessed, locally-sourced ingredients; free from refined sugars and unnecessary additives. All food is prepared on-site: In the Nurture kitchen you can find dough rising, bread baking, beans soaking, piles of fresh produce, and meat slow-cooking. The Kitchen Café is a safe, inclusive and pleasant eating environment, where young minds are nourished, family-style eating behaviours are encouraged, and positive social eating habits are developed.[1]

ABOUT THE SETTING

Nurture Early Learning is a Reggio-inspired group of childcare centres for children aged between six months and five years. It is a growing chain, with two centres currently open and another four in the pipeline. About a year ago, Anya began changing how meal and snack times worked at Nurture in Auckland, where she cooks for 75 children. The changes worked so well that Anya's approach has been adopted as part of the Nurture brand. She will be instrumental in rolling this out across their other childcare centres.

I asked Anya about what meal and snack times look like at her setting, what the challenges have been in terms of making changes and what impact the new way of doing things has had on the children who attend the setting. She also gave me a bit of context in relation to cultural norms in New Zealand. The ideas Anya espouses are better known in the USA but, in New Zealand, they are unheard of. As in the UK, controlling feeding practices are often used and little is known about how to help children self-regulate. Rolling mealtimes are fashionable in childcare settings in New Zealand, on the basis that they show respect to children. This is at odds with the importance of structure that Anya teaches. Anya told me that her evidence-based approach to feeding is simply not on the radar in New Zealand.

MEALTIMES AT NURTURE

Family-style serving is used and staff are taught to empower children to make their own eating decisions in line with the division of responsibility. At snack time, foods (at least three things: a fruit, a vegetable and a protein source) are served together on a tray. The quantity available is based on age-appropriate portion sizes but children are allowed to serve themselves. Anya works with a four-week seasonal menu plan that is changed four times a year. Anya says:

> You put everything on one tray, two pairs of tongs and off you go! No 'You must eat this, you must eat that…'

The pre-schoolers' lunch is also served family-style, with the children eating on small tables of six to eight. The children are learning to pour their own water from jugs and all children are encouraged to take an active part in meals, helping set the table and clear away.

Staff have been taught not to see it as their role to persuade children to eat or try foods. Instead, they work to foster a supportive and positive eating environment where children are engaged with their food and are learning to eat in response to their bodies rather than because of the adults around them.

PARENTS

Anya understands the importance of working with parents. I asked her what they make of the way she does things, and she replied that they are more aware of the food than the feeding practices.

What parents talk about is what the children are eating when they attend the setting, or how a child who is picky at home eats so well in day care. They are very supportive of Anya's way of doing things because they see the end results. Parents have even commented that their child isn't getting ill any more, now they're eating such a varied diet.

Anya believes that the best way to work with parents is through training opportunities. She runs a series of workshops for parents, covering all sorts of things including cooking and picky eating. Anya makes sure that she includes resources from other professionals in her workshops, so that parents understand that this is not just something she has made up!

CHALLENGES

There were many challenges for Anya when she brought in the new way of doing things. For years, staff had been used to persuading children to eat everything on their plates, to push them to try things, to praise them when they ate something. Anya can relate to this. She explained how, when she came across these ideas for the first time, she was incredulous:

> When I was first introduced to these ideas four years ago, my first thought was 'You've got to be kidding me! It's already a performance out there, how is this going to make things better?!'

She understands that it takes time for staff to fully adopt a new approach. They are being asked to do things that challenge culturally established ways of doing things and this is really hard. They are also unlikely to have encountered these ideas as part of their training. Anya explains that training for educators (early years practitioners) involves some superficial information about nutrition, but 'doesn't talk about how you're going to sit the children down and feed them!' She says, 'I ask them, has anyone ever mentioned the division of responsibility? And they look at me blankly.'

EMBEDDING GOOD FEEDING PRACTICES IN A SETTING

Anya shared some suggestions about how to achieve this, based on her experience.

Repeat the message

Anya described how it can take a long time for old habits to fade away. This is not an overnight revolution and staff won't get it right all of the time. She explained that:

> When it doesn't work, this is either because staff are not role modelling or they are still putting pressure on.

Feedback needs to be delivered sensitively and staff need to be reminded about what is expected in the context of effective training.

Understand the cultural perspective of colleagues

Anya explained how some of her colleagues are from Pacific Island communities and food is a big part of their culture. It is culturally normal to give big servings and colleagues have articulated to Anya how hard they find letting children make their own eating decisions and not serving large portions. One educator told Anya, 'I find this so hard to do because we just don't do it in our culture.' If we can create a safe space for these conversations to take place, an awareness of cultural norms is the first step towards the successful adoption of new practices.

Get management onside

Anya described how the Nurture management and owners are supportive of her work, but that it was important to give them the rationale for the changes she has made. She has shared training materials with them when she has attended courses, and has made sure they appreciate that this is an evidence-based approach, underpinned by a substantial body of research.

Appreciate the importance of practitioners' own relationships with food

Anya talked about potential struggles where colleagues' eating behaviours were perhaps problematic. She is not sure how to work with this but knows that it is key, explaining:

> People's own history is a factor. And I don't really know how to deal with that, apart from I am aware of it.

Anya has tapped into the way in which our approaches to feeding children are tied to our own eating. If we feel guilty that our diet is far from ideal, or that we are unable to effectively self-regulate, it is very hard to support children's self-regulation.

Strive for consistent training

Anya has found that there has sometimes been a lack of clarity around whose responsibility it is to explain to new staff how things are done: the teacher's, or hers. This has led her to work towards a more structured induction system for new staff. She is especially mindful that relief staff may not have attended her workshops and it's essential to ensure that good practice is understood by everyone who is involved with feeding children.

The quality of training has to be consistent too: ideas can become misunderstood and watered down. For example, the division of responsibility can be taken to mean that a child gets to make their own eating decisions and so can opt to have strawberry ice cream for breakfast!

OUTCOMES

I was very interested to learn about the impact of the changes Anya has brought in at Nurture. Here are some of the things she says have changed.

More support for picky eaters

Once the eating environment is right and mealtimes are relaxed, positive and pressure-free, it becomes much easier to see who the genuinely picky eaters are and to support them in a more focused way:

> One thing I've said to the girls [centre staff] is if we can get them eating nicely this way, then we can really target the ones who are picky eaters and then you've got options from there, whereas when it's all bedlam, as far as they're concerned, they're all picky eaters! Of course, they're not. It's just that the environment isn't right.

Children eat more good food

Anya has noticed that children are happily eating a wider variety of nutritious food now that they are trusted to make their own eating decisions in a pressure-free environment.

Children voluntarily try food

Children feel in control and relaxed during meals and Anya has seen that they are far more likely to try new foods in a positive eating environment.

Children make healthy choices

Parents report that children make healthy choices by themselves outside of the setting.

Educators can enjoy mealtimes

Staff can make positive use of their time with children at meal and snack times because they are not taking on the role of policing what and how much is eaten.

There are so many advantages to using evidence-based good feeding practices in early years settings, but change doesn't happen overnight. Anya says:

> To bring people round takes time. I know I will have to keep plugging away. I talk a lot about building that relationship between the educator and the child, and the child and the food. It gets them thinking…

Anya Bell is active on social media as Anya's Real Food Kitchen.

FINAL THOUGHTS

Thank you for taking the time to read this book. I have tried to introduce you to an evidence-based approach to feeding children which is not widely known about in the UK. The central goal of this approach is to support children's ability to self-regulate. This is at the heart of a positive relationship with food. Underpinning self-regulation, though, are the notions of trust and respect. I'd like to conclude by talking a bit about each of these.

TRUST

We know that, if we can create the right structure and environment (and of course, provide the right food), we can leave children to tune in to their physical signals and eat in response to these. We don't need to take on the role of persuading children to eat and we don't need to feel in charge of their food intake. When children trust us to provide good food and we trust them to get on with eating it, something magical happens. They begin to trust themselves.

RESPECT

Providing good food for children is a huge part of respecting them. We need to respect their ability to enjoy good food if they have been taught to do so. We need to respect their right to be provided with nutritious, tasty food every single day. Children do not deserve a lesser, blander (and often unhealthier) range of foods than adults. With the right support, they can engage with a varied and exciting diet. Our job is to give them the skills and environment which will facilitate this.

Not only do we need to respect children, we need to model respect for our bodies and what we eat. It is essential to help children engage with their food, learning about where it comes from and why we need it. We need to teach a joyful and connected approach to eating, which children will take with them long after they have moved beyond early years.

WHAT YOU CAN DO

Adopting evidence-based best practice in relation to feeding children is really hard. This is because you may feel like you are swimming against the tide as you challenge social and cultural norms. It is also incredibly rewarding. Once you have a thorough understanding of how to feed children in a way that supports a positive relationship with food, you will be able to embed this in everything you do as a setting: in your entire ethos. The early years are such an important time in the formation of positive habits and the optimisation of health outcomes for children. You can truly make a difference.

Resources

FEEDING CHILDREN (AND CHILDHOOD NUTRITION)

Albon, D. and Mukherji, P. (2008) *Food and Health in Early Childhood: A Holistic Approach.* Los Angeles, CA: Sage.

Rose, J., Gilbert, L. and Richards, V. (2016) 'Nutrition in health and wellbeing' in *Health and Well-being in Early Childhood.* London: Sage.

Underdown, A. (2007) 'Growth and nutrition' in *Young Children's Health and Well-being.* Maidenhead: McGraw-Hill/Open University Press.

British Nutrition Foundation – lots of nutrition-related resources, including wall posters. www.nutrition.org.uk

The Child Feeding Guide – advice and resources from academics at Loughborough University. www.childfeedingguide.co.uk

The Infant and Toddler Forum – evidence-based advice and guidance for child health. www.infantandtoddlerforum.org

COOKING SKILLS FOR FAMILIES

Scotland, S. *What a family needs to know about eating well and being clever with food.* (This is a booklet you can purchase to share with parents, from www.sarah-scotland.co.uk.)

FOOD AND CULTURAL IDENTITY

Albon, D. and Mukherji, P. (2008) 'Food, culture and identity' in *Food and Health in Early Childhood: A Holistic Approach.* Los Angeles, CA: Sage. This provides an excellent exploration of the cultural significance of what we eat.

GOVERNMENT RESOURCES

The Eatwell Guide (which replaced the Eatwell Plate in 2016) – UK Government recommendations regarding a balanced diet. www.gov.uk/government/publications/the-eatwell-guide

SPECIAL CASES

Supporting picky eaters

Rowell, K. and McGlothin, J. (2015) *Helping Your Child with Extreme Picky Eating: A Step-by-Step Guide for Overcoming Selective Eating, Food Aversion, and Feeding Disorders.* Oakland, CA: New Harbinger Publications.

Allergies

Recob, A. (2009) *The BugaBees: Friends with Food Allergies.* Edina, MN: Beavers Pond Press.

Oral motor skills

Brackett, K. (2016) *When Your Child Can't or Won't Eat: A Guide for Parents and Caregivers of Children with Feeding and Eating Disorders.* (This is an e-book available from www.pediatricfeedingnews.com.)

Sensory processing

Abraham, D., Heffron, C., Brayley, P. and Drobnjak, L. (2015) *Sensory Processing 101.* (This is an e-book and paperback available from www.sensoryprocessing101.com and online book retailers.)

Looked after and adopted children

Rowell, K. (2012) *Love Me, Feed Me: The Adoptive Parent's Guide to Ending the Worry About Weight, Picky Eating, Power Struggles and More.* St Paul, MN: Family Feeding Dynamics, LLC. (This book is aimed at parents but is full of information which is also relevant to practitioners.)

RESOURCES FROM THE CHILDREN'S FOOD TRUST

Visit www.childrensfoodtrust.org.uk for a wide range of resources including:

- producing and sharing allergen information
- developing a food policy
- healthy packed lunches

- catering for special dietary requirement

- example menus

- food label cards.

The following documents from the Children's Food Trust are essential reading:

Voluntary Food and Drink Guidelines for Early Years Settings in England: A Practical Guide (2012)

Promoting and Supporting Healthy Eating in Early Years Settings: A Guide for Early Years Settings in England (2015)

Healthy Packed Lunches for Early Years: A Practical Guide for Parents and Carers (2016)

TRAINING RESOURCES

The University of Idaho provides many resources related to feeding children in group settings, for both trainers and practitioners. www.cals.uidaho.edu/feeding

See the Ellyn Satter Institute website for details of Satter's work, including training resources. www.ellynsatterinstitute.org

HENRY provides practitioner training relating to childhood obesity. www.henry.org.uk

PLANNING

Barber, J. (2012) *Planning for the Early Years: Food and Cooking.* London: Practical Pre-school Books.

Bryce-Clegg, A. (2012) *Planning for the Early Years: Gardening and Growing.* London: Practical Pre-school Books.

References

Albon, D. (2009). Challenges to improving the uptake of milk in a nursery class: a case study. *Health Education*, 109(2), 140–154.

American Psychiatric Association (2013). *Diagnostic and Statistical Manual of Mental Disorders, Fifth Edition*. Arlington, VA: American Psychiatric Association.

Anderson, S. and Keim, S. (2016). Parent–child interaction, self-regulation, and obesity prevention in early childhood. *Current Obesity Reports*, 5(2), 192–200.

Ayres, A. and Robbins, J. (2005). *Sensory Integration and the Child: Understanding Hidden Sensory Challenges*. Los Angeles, CA: Western Psychological Services.

Birch, L., Marlin, D. and Rotter, J. (1984). Eating as the 'means' activity in a contingency: effects on young children's food preference. *Child Development*, 431–439.

Birch, L. Savage.L and Ventura, S. (2007). Influences on the development of children's eating behaviours: from infancy to adolescence. *Canadian Journal of Dietetic Practice and Research : A Publication of Dietitians of Canada*, 68(1), s1–s56.

Blissett, J. and Haycraft, E. (2008). Are parenting style and controlling feeding practices related? *Appetite*, 50(2), 477–485.

Brackett, K. (2016). When Your Child Can't or Won't Eat: A Guide for Parents and Caregivers of Children with Feeding and Eating Disorders. Accessed on 08/08/2017 at http://pediatricfeedingnews.com/product/when-your-child-cant-or-wont-eat

Branen, L., Fletcher, J. and Myers, L. (1997). Effects of pre-portioned and family-style food service on preschool children's food intake and waste at snacktime, *Journal of Research in Childhood Education*, 12(1), 88–95.

Bryant-Waugh, R. (2013). Avoidant restrictive food intake disorder: an illustrative case example. *International Journal of Eating Disorders*, 46, 420–423.

Buck, D. (2016) The Childhood Obesity Plan: Brave and bold action? Accessed on 08/08/2017 at https://www.kingsfund.org.uk/blog/2016/08/childhood-obesity-plan

Busick, D., Brooks, J., Pernecky, S., Dawson, R. and Petzoldt, J. (2008). Parent food purchases as a measure of exposure and preschool-aged children's willingness to identify and taste fruit and vegetables. *Appetite*, 51(3), 468–73.

Cardona Cano, S., Hoek, H., Van Hoeken, D., Barse, L. *et al.* (2016). Behavioral outcomes of picky eating in childhood: a prospective study in the general population. *Journal of Child Psychology and Psychiatry*, 57(11), 1239–1246.

Cardona Cano, S., Tiemeier, H., Van Hoeken, D., Tharner, A. *et al.* (2015). Trajectories of picky eating during childhood: a general population study. *International Journal of Eating Disorders*, 48, 6, 570–579.

Carruth, B., Skinner, J., Houck, K., Moran III, J., Coletta, F. and Ott, D. (1998). The phenomenon of 'picky eater': a behavioral marker in eating patterns of toddlers. *Journal of the American College of Nutrition*, 17(2), 180–186.

Cermak, S., Curtin, C. and Bandini, L. (2010). Food selectivity and sensory sensitivity in children with autism spectrum disorders. *Journal of the American Dietetic Association*, 110(2), 238–246.

Chatoor, I. (2002). Feeding disorders in infants and toddlers. *Child and Adolescent Psychiatric Clinics of North America*, 11, 63–183.

Children's Food Trust (2012a). *Eat Better, Start Better. Voluntary Food and Drink Guidelines for Early Years Settings in England – A Practical Guide.* Accessed on 01/04/2017 at http://media.childrensfoodtrust.org.uk/2015/06/CFT_Early_Years_Guide_Interactive_Sept-12.pdf

Children's Food Trust (2012b). *Example food policy and step by step guide to producing a policy.* Accessed on 18/10/2017 at www.childrensfoodtrust.org.uk/childrens-food-trust/early-years/ey-resources

Children's Food Trust (2015a). *Catering for Special Dietary Requirements: A Guide for Early Years Settings in England.* Accessed on 17/05/2017 at http://media.childrensfoodtrust.org.uk/2015/11/CFT-Early-Years-Special-diets-Factsheet.pdf

Children's Food Trust (2015b). *Promoting and Supporting Healthy Eating in Early Years Settings.* Accessed on 01/04/2017 at http://media.childrensfoodtrust.org.uk/2015/11/CFT-Early-Years-Promoting-Supporting-Healthy-Eating.pdf

Children's Food Trust (2015c). *Healthy Packed Lunches for Early Years: A Practical Guide for Parents and Carers.* Accessed on 06/11/2017 at http://media.childrensfoodtrust.org.uk/2015/05/CFT-Packed-Lunch-Guidance.pdf

Cockroft, J., Durkin, M., Masding, C. and Cade, J. (2005). Fruit and vegetable intakes in a sample of pre-school children participating in the 'Five for All' project in Bradford. *Public Health Nutrition*, 8(7), 861–9.

Cooke, L. (2007). The importance of exposure for healthy eating in childhood: a review. *Journal of Human Nutrition and Dietetics*, 20(4), 294–301.

Cormack, J. (2015). They may not be big, but they are clever (Emotionally Aware Feeding blog). Accessed on 08/08/2017 at www.emotionallyawarefeeding.com/blog/2015/7/26/they-may-not-be-big-but-they-are-clever-my-interview-with-sara-keel

Costanzo, P. and Woody, E. (1985). Domain-specific parenting styles and their impact on the child's development of particular deviance: the example of obesity proneness. *Journal of Social and Clinical Psychology*, 3(4), 425–445.

Coulthard, H. and Blissett, J. (2009). Fruit and vegetable consumption in children and their mothers: moderating effects of child sensory sensitivity. *Appetite*, 52(2), 410–415.

Daniels, A. and Mandell, D. (2014). Explaining differences in age at autism spectrum disorder diagnosis: a critical review. *Autism*, 18(5), 583–597.

DfE (Department for Education) (2017) Statutory Framework for the Early Years Foundation Stage: Setting the Standards for Learning, Development and Care for Children from Birth to Five. Accessed on 02/06/2017 at www.foundationyears.org.uk/files/2017/03/EYFS_STATUTORY_FRAMEWORK_2017.pdf

Dimbleby, H. and Vincent, J. (2013). The School Food Plan. Accessed on 17/07/2017 at www.schoolfoodplan.com/wp-content/uploads/2013/07/School_Food_Plan_2013.pdf

Dovey, T., Staples, P., Gibson, L. and Halford, J. (2008). Food neophobia and 'picky/fussy' eating in children: a review. *Appetite*, 50(2/3), 181–193.

Estrem, H., Pados, B., Park, J., Knafl, K. and Thoyre, S. (2017). Feeding problems in infancy and early childhood: evolutionary concept analysis. *Journal of Advanced Nursing*, 73(1), 56–70.

Farrow, C. and Coulthard, H. (2012) Relationships between sensory sensitivity, anxiety and selective eating in children. *Appetite*, 58,(3), 842–846.

Farrow, C., Haycraft, E. and Blissett, J. (2015) Teaching our children when to eat: how parental feeding practices inform the development of emotional eating – a longitudinal experimental design. *American Journal of Clinical Nutrition*,101, 908–13.

Fisher, M., Rosen, D. Ornstein, R., Mammel, K. *et al.* (2014). Characteristics of avoidant/restrictive food intake disorder in children and adolescents: a 'new disorder' in DSM-5. *Journal of Adolescent Health*, 55(1), 49–52.

Fraker, C., Walbert, L., Cox, S. and Fishbein, M. (2009). *Food Chaining: The Proven 6-Step Plan to Stop Picky Eating, Solve Feeding Problems, and Expand your Child's Diet.* Cambridge, MA: Perseus Books.

Godsey, J. (2013). The role of mindfulness based interventions in the treatment of obesity and eating disorders: an integrative review. *Complementary Therapies in Medicine*, 21(4), 430–9.

Goossens, L., Braet, C., Van Vlierberghe, L. and Mels, S. (2009). Loss of control over eating in overweight youngsters: the role of anxiety, depression and emotional eating. *European Eating Disorders Review*, 17(1), 68–78.

HM Government (2017) *Childhood Obesity: A Plan for Action.* Accessed on 28/06/2017 at https://www.gov.uk/government/publications/childhood-obesity-a-plan-for-action/childhood-obesity-a-plan-for-action

Hope, C. (2015). Teachers can lawfully 'confiscate, keep or destroy' unhealthy lunchbox snacks, ministers say. Accessed on 07/05/2017 at www.telegraph.co.uk/news/politics/11711699/Teachers-can-lawfully-confiscate-keep-or-destroy-unhealthy-lunchbox-snacks-ministers-say.html

Houston-Price, C., Butler, L. and Shiba, P. (2009). Visual exposure impacts on toddlers' willingness to taste fruits and vegetables. *Appetite,* 53(3), 450–453.

Howard, A., Mallan, K., Byrne, R., Magarey, A. and Daniels, L. (2012). Toddlers' food preferences: the impact of novel food exposure, maternal preferences and food neophobia. *Appetite, 59*(3), 818–825.

Infant and Toddler Forum (2010). Toddler Meals: How Much Do They Need? Accessed on 15/05/2017 at www.infantandtoddlerforum.org/media/upload/pdf-downloads/1.7_-_Toddler_meals_-_how_much_do_they_need.pdf

Jackson, D. and Mannix, J. (2004). Giving voice to the burden of blame: a feminist study of mothers' experiences of mother blaming. *International Journal of Nursing Practice,* 10(4), 150–158.

Jacobsen, M. (2016). *From Picky to Powerful: The Mindset, Strategies and Know-How You Need to Empower Your Picky Eater.* USA: RMI Books.

Johansson, S., Bieber, T., Dahl, R., Friedmann, P. *et al.* (2004). Revised nomenclature for allergy for global use: report of the Nomenclature Review Committee of the World Allergy Organization, October 2003. *The Journal of Allergy and Clinical Immunology,* 113(5), 832–836.

Kelly, A. and Rhodes, P. (2013). The evolution of the DSM and some implications for clinicians' practice. *Clinical Psychology Forum,* 243, 28–31.

Kenny, L., Hattersley, C., Molins, B., Buckley, C., Povey, C. and Pellicano, E. (2015). Which terms should be used to describe autism? Perspectives from the UK autism community, *Autism,* 20(4), 442–462.

Kohn, A. (2000). *Punished by Rewards: The Trouble with Gold Stars, Incentive Plans, A's, Praise and Other Bribes.* New York: Houghton Mifflin.

Lee, C. (1990). *The Growth and Development of Children,* 4th edn. Longman: London and New York, 118.

Leung, A., Marchand, V. and Sauve, R. (2012). The 'picky eater': the toddler or preschooler who does not eat. *Paediatric Child Health,* 17(8), 455–457.

Lipps Birch, L. and Deysher, M. (1985) Conditioned and unconditioned caloric compensation: evidence for self-regulation of food intake in young children. Learning and Motivation, 16(3).

Lomer, M. (2015). Review article: the aetiology, diagnosis, mechanisms and clinical evidence for food intolerance. *Alimentary Pharmacology & Therapeutics,* 41(3), 262–275.

Machado, B., Dias, P., Lima, V., Campos, J. and Goncalves, S. (2016) Prevalence and correlates of picky eating in preschool-aged children: a population-based study. *Journal of Eating Behaviors,* 22, 16–21.

Manno, C., Fox, C., Eicher, P. and Kerwin, M. (2005). Early oral-motor interventions for pediatric feeding problems: what, when and how. *Journal of Early and Intensive Behavior Intervention,* 2(3), 145–159.

Maslow, A. (1943). A theory of human motivation. *Psychological Review,* 50, 370–396.

Mennella, J., Spector, A., Reed, D., and Coldwell, S. (2013). The bad taste of medicines: overview of basic research on bitter taste. *Clinical Therapeutics,* 35(8), 1225–46.

Micali, N., Simonoff, E., Stahl, D. and Treasure, J. (2011). Maternal eating disorders and infant feeding difficulties: maternal and child mediators in a longitudinal general population study. *Journal of Child Psychology and Psychiatry,* 52(7), 800–807.

Miller, L., Nielsen, D., Schoen, S. and Brett-Green, B. (2009). Perspectives on sensory processing disorder: a call for translational research. *Frontiers in Integrative Neuroscience,* 3.

Mintel (2016). Britons lose count of their calories: over a third of Brits don't know how many calories they consume on a typical day. Accessed on 08/08/2017 at www.mintel.com/press-centre/food-and-drink/brits-lose-count-of-their-calories-over-a-third-of-brits-dont-know-how-many-calories-they-consume-on-a-typical-day

Mortlock, A. (2015). Toddlers' use of peer rituals at mealtime: symbols of togetherness and otherness. *International Journal of Early Years Education*, 23(4), 426–435.

Muraro, A., Agache, I., Clark, A., Sheikh, A. *et al.* (2014). EAACI Food Allergy and Anaphylaxis Guidelines: managing patients with food allergy in the community. *Allergy: European Journal of Allergy and Clinical Immunology*, 69(8), 1046–1057.

Nadon, G., Feldman, D., Dunn, W. and Gisel, E. (2011). Association of sensory processing and eating problems in children with autism spectrum disorders. *Autism Research and Treatment*, 2011.

National Statistics (2016). *Statistics on Obesity, Physical Activity and Diet.* Accessed on 28/06/2017 at http://content.digital.nhs.uk/catalogue/PUB20562/obes-phys-acti-diet-eng-2016-rep.pdf

Nicholls, D., Chater, R. and Lask, B. (2000). Children into DSM don't go: a comparison of classification systems for eating disorders in childhood and early adolescence. *The International Journal of Eating Disorders*, 28(3), 317–24.

Nordström, K., Coff, C., Jönsson, H., Nordenfelt, L. and Görman, U. (2013). Food and health: individual, cultural, or scientific matters? *Genes & Nutrition*, 8(4), 357–363.

Nwaru, B., Hickstein, L., Panesar, S., Roberts, G., Muraro, A. and Sheikh, A. (2014). Prevalence of common food allergies in Europe: a systematic review and meta-analysis. *Allergy*, 69(8), 992–1007.

Odar Stough, C., Dreyer Gillette, M., Roberts, M., Jorgensen, T. and Patton, S. (2015). Mealtime behaviors associated with consumption of unfamiliar foods by young children with autism spectrum disorder. *Appetite*, 95, 324–333.

Ofsted (2015a). *Common Inspection Framework: Education, Skills and Early Years.* Accessed 01/08/2017 at https://www.gov.uk/government/uploads/system/uploads/attachment_data/file/461767/The_common_inspection_framework_education_skills_and_early_years.pdf

Ofsted (2015b). *Early Years Inspection Handbook.* Accessed on 02/04/2017 at https://www.gov.uk/government/publications/early-years-inspection-handbook-from-september-2015

PACEY (2016). Children as young as 3 unhappy with their bodies. Accessed on 08/08/2017 at https://www.pacey.org.uk/news-and-views/news/archive/2016-news/august-2016/children-as-young-as-3-unhappy-with-their-bodies

Paul, S., Kirkham, E., Pidgeon, S. and Sandmann, S. (2015). Coeliac disease in children. *Nursing Standard (royal College of Nursing (Great Britain)*, 29(49), 36–41.

Peeters, A., Barendregt, J., Willekens, F., Mackenbach, J., Al Mamun, A. and Bonneux, L. (2003). Obesity in adulthood and its consequences for life expectancy: a life-table analysis. *Annals of Internal Medicine*, 138(1), 24–32.

Powell, F., Farrow, C. and Meyer, C. (2011). Food avoidance in children: the influence of maternal feeding practices and behaviours. *Appetite*, 57, 683–92.

Price, D. (2008). *Pediatric Nursing: An Introductory Text*, 10th edn. MI: Saunders Elsevier.Remington, A., Añfez, E., Croker, H., Wardle, J. and Cooke, L. (2012) Increasing food acceptance in the home setting: a randomized controlled trial of parent-administered taste exposure with incentives. American Journal of Clinical Nutrition, 99(1), 72–77.

Ricca, V., Castellini, G., Sauro, C., Ravaldi, C. *et al.* (2009). Correlations between binge eating and emotional eating in a sample of overweight subjects. *Appetite*, 53(3), 418–421.

Robinson, M. (2008). *Child Development 0–8: A Journey through the Early Years.* Maidenhead: Open University Press.

Rose, D. (2014). *It's Not About the Broccoli: Three Habits to Teach Your Kids for a Lifetime of Healthy Eating.* New York: Penguin Publishing Group.

Rowell, K. (2012). *Love Me, Feed Me.* St Paul, MN: Family Feeding Dynamics, LLC.

Rowell, K. and McGlothlin, J. (2015). Helping Your Child with Extreme Picky Eating: A Step-by-Step Guide for Overcoming Selective Eating, Food Aversion, and Feeding Disorders. Oakland, CA: New Harbinger Publications.

Satter, E. (2000). *Child of Mine: Feeding with Love and Good Sense.* Boulder, CO: James Bull.

Satter, E. (2007). Eating competence: definition and evidence for the Satter Eating Competence Model. *Journal of Nutrition Education and Behavior*, Supplement, 39, 5.

Skinner, J., Carruth, B., Bounds, W. and Ziegler, P. (2002). Children's food preferences: a longitudinal analysis. *Journal of the American Dietetic Association*, 102(11), 1638–1647.

Skinner, J., Ruth, C., Moran, J., Houck, K. *et al.* (1998). Toddlers' food preferences: concordance with family members' preferences. *Journal of Nutrition Education*, 30, 1, 17–22.

Smith, A., Herle, M., Fildes, A., Cooke, L., Steinsbekk, S. and Llewellyn, C. (2017). Food fussiness and food neophobia share a common etiology in early childhood. *Journal of Child Psychology and Psychiatry*, 58(2), 189–196.

Stegenga, H., Haines, A., Jones, K., Wilding, J. and Guideline Development Group (2014). Identification, assessment, and management of overweight and obesity: summary of updated NICE guidance. *British Medical Journal*, 349, g6608.

Tanofsky-Kraff, M., Theim, K., Yanovski, S., Bassett, A. *et al.* (2007). Validation of the emotional eating scale adapted for use in children and adolescents (EES-C). *The International Journal of Eating Disorders*, 40(3), 232–40.

Tanofsky-Kraff, M., Yanovski, S., Schvey, N., Olsen, C., Gustafson, J. and Yanovski, J. (2009). A prospective study of loss of control eating for body weight gain in children at high risk for adult obesity. *International Journal of Eating Disorders*, 42(1), 26–30.

Taylor, C., Wernimont, S., Northstone, K., Emmett, P. (2015). Picky/fussy eating in children: review of definitions, assessment, prevalence and dietary intakes. *Appetite*, 95, 349–59

Tharner, A., Jansen, P., Kiefte-de Jong, J., Moll, H. *et al.* (2014). Toward an operative diagnosis of fussy/picky eating: a latent profile approach in a population-based cohort. *International Journal of Behavioral Nutrition and Physical Activity*, 11(14).

The Requirements for School Food Regulations (2014). SI 2014/1603. Accessed on 08/08/2017 at www.legislation.gov.uk/uksi/2014/1603/pdfs/uksi_20141603_en.pdf

Tobin, B. (2015) Over a third of Brits are unhappy with their bodies. Accessed on 07/08/2017 at https://yougov.co.uk/news/2015/07/21/over-third-brits-unhappy-their-bodies-celebrity-cu

Trussel Trust (2017). Year end statistics. Accessed on 08/08/2017 at https://www.trusselltrust.org/news-and-blog/latest-stats/end-year-stats

Van Strien, T. and Oosterveld, P. (2008). The children's DEBQ for assessment of restrained, emotional, and external eating in 7-to 12-year-old children. *International Journal of Eating Disorders*, 41(1), 72–81.

Webster Stratton, C. (2006). *The Incredible Years*. The Incredible Years.

Williams, L. (2017). *Positive Behaviour Management in Early Years Settings: An Essential Guide*. London: Jessica Kingsley Publishers.

World Health Organization (1992). *The ICD-10 Classification of Mental and Behavioural Disorders: Clinical Descriptions and Diagnostic Guidelines*. Geneva: World Health Organization.

Wright, C., Parkinson, K. and Drewett, R. (2006) How does maternal and child feeding behavior relate to weight gain and failure to thrive? Data from a prospective birth cohort. *Pediatrics*, 117(4), 1262–9.

Yochman, A., Parush, S. and Ornoy, A. (2004). Responses of preschool children with and without ADHD to sensory events in daily life. *American Journal of Occupational Therapy*, 58, 294–302.

Vaughn, A., Ward, D., Fisher, J., Faith, M. *et al.* (2016). Fundamental constructs in food parenting practices: a content map to guide future research, *Nutrition Reviews*, 74(2), 98–117.

Wiley, D. and Cory, A. (2013). *Encyclopedia of School Health*. Thousand Oaks, CA: Sage, 11.

Zimmer, M., Desch, L., Rosen, L., Bailey, M. et al. (2012). Sensory integration therapies for children with developmental and behavioural disorders. *Pediatrics*, 129(6), 1186–9.

Zopf, Y., Hahn, E., Raithel, M., Baenkler, H. and Silbermann, A. (2009). The differential diagnosis of food intolerance. *Deutches Artzblatt International*, 106(21), 359–370.

Zucker, N., Copeland, W., Franz, L., Carpenter, K. *et al.* (2015). Psychological and psychosocial impairment in preschoolers with selective eating. *Pediatrics*, 136(3), 582–90.

Notes

Introduction

1. Dovey *et al.*, 2008
2. See the Change4Life Programme at https://campaignresources.phe.gov.uk/resources/campaigns/17-change4life/overview
3. Dovey *et al.*, 2008

Chapter 1

1. Maslow, 1943
2. Wiley and Cory, 2013, p.11
3. Birch, Savage and Ventura, 2007
4. Smith *et al.*, 2017
5. Skinner *et al.*, 2002
6. Cockroft *et al.*, 2005

Chapter 2

1. Kohn, 2000
2. Satter, 2007
3. Rowell, 2012
4. Anderson and Keim, 2016

Chapter 3

1. Satter, 2000
2. Satter, 2000, p.3, italics added

Chapter 4

1. Skinner *et al.*, 1998
2. Todhunter, cited in Skinner *et al.*, 1998, p.17
3. Busick *et al.*, 2008
4. Cooke, 2007
5. Cooke, 2007, p.299
6. Howard *et al.*, 2012
7. Carruth *et al.*, 1998

Chapter 5

1. Smith *et al.*, 2017
2. Vaughn *et al.*, 2016
3. Blissett and Haycraft, 2008
4. At Penn State University, USA
5. Birch, 1982, cited in: Carruth *et al.*, 1998
6. Birch, Marlin and Rotter, 1984

Chapter 6

1. Zucker *et al.*, 2015
2. Costanzo and Woody, 1985
3. Wright, Parkinson and Drewett, 2006

Chapter 7

1. Webster Stratton, 2006
2. Remington *et al.*, 2012
3. Rowell and McGlothlin, 2015, p.84

Chapter 8

1. Price, 2008
2. Leung, Marchand and Sauve, 2012
3. Leung *et al.*, 2012, p.455
4. Lipps, Birch, and Deysher, 1985

Chapter 9

1. Tanofsky-Kraff *et al.*, 2007
2. Farrow, Haycraft and Blissett, 2015
3. Tanofsky-Kraff *et al.*, 2009
4. Goossens *et al.*, 2009
5. Ricca *et al.*, 2009
6. Godsey, 2013
7. Godsey, 2013, p.438
8. Goossens *et al.*, 2009

Chapter 10

1. Powell, Farrow and Meyer, 2011

Chapter 11

1. PACEY, 2016
2. Mintel, 2016

Chapter 12

1. See Tobin, 2015

Chapter 13

1. Infant and Toddler Forum, 2010
2. Children's Food Trust, 2012a

Chapter 14

1. DfE, 2017
2. Children's Food Trust, 2012a
3. Dimbleby and Vincent, 2003
4. *The Requirements for School Food Regulations*, 2014
5. Children's Food Trust, 2012a
6. *The Requirents for School Food Regulations*, 2014

Chapter 15

1. Jacobsen, 2016, p.42
2. Rowell and McGlothlin, 2015, p.119
3. Branen, Fletcher and Myers, 1997
4. Branen *et al.*, 1997

Chapter 16

1. Dimbleby and Vincent, 2013, p.84

Chapter 17

1. Carruth *et al.*,1998
2. Williams, 2017, p.52
3. Farrow and Coulthard, 2012
4. Coulthard and Blissett, 2009
5. Yochman, Parush and Ornoy, 2004
6. Van Strien and Oosterveld, 2008

Chapter 18

1. Lee, 1990, p.118
2. DfE, 2017
3. DfE, 2017, p.8
4. Mortlock, 2015

Chapter 19

1. Williams, 2017
2. Rose, 2014, p.240

Chapter 20

1. DfE, 2017, p.11
2. Nordström *et al.*, 2013, p.358
3. Ofsted, 2015a
4. Ofsted, 2015b
5. Children's Food Trust, 2015b, p.1
6. DfE, 2017, p.8
7. Children's Food Trust, 2015b

Chapter 22

1. Children's Food Trust, 2012b
2. Children's Food Trust, 2012a
3. Mucavele, 2017, personal correspondence
4. DfE, 2017, 3.73
5. Hope, 2015.
6. Dimbleby and Vincent, 2013
7. Dimbleby and Vincent, 2013, p.136
8. Dimbleby and Vincent, 2013, p.68
9. Children's Food Trust, 2012a, p.52
10. Children's Food Trust, 2015c

Chapter 24

1. Jackson and Mannix, 2004, p.150
2. Micali, Simonoff, Stahl and Treasure, 2011

Chapter 25

1. See www.nhs.uk/Tools/Pages/birthtofive. aspx
2. Maslow, 1943

Chapter 26

1. Children's Food Trust, 2012a
2. See www.nurserymilk.co.uk
3. Albon, 2009
4. Children's Food Trust, 2012a, p.26
5. Cormack, 2015

Chapter 27

1. Houston-Price, Butler and Shiba, 2009

Chapter 28

1. Cockroft *et al.*, 2005, p.868
2. Trussel Trust, 2017

Chapter 29

1. Tharner *et al.*, 2014
2. Vaughn *et al.*, 2016
3. Taylor *et al.*, 2015
4. Machado *et al.*, 2016
5. Cardona Cano *et al.*, 2015

6. Cardona Cano *et al.*, 2016
7. Cardona Cano *et al.*, 2015
8. Cardona Cano *et al.*, 2015, p.575
9. Jacobsen, 2016, p.24
10. Fraker *et al.*, 2009
11. Jacobsen, 2016, p.6

Chapter 30

1. Taylor *et al.*, 2015
2. Mennella *et al.*, 2013
3. From Robinson, 2008, pp.189–190
4. Farrow and Coulthard, 2012

Chapter 31

1. Satter, 2000

Chapter 32

1. Fraker *et al.*, 2009

Chapter 33

1. World Health Organization, 1992
2. American Psychiatric Association, 2013
3. Kelly and Rhodes, 2013
4. Estrem *et al.*, 2017
5. Bryant-Waugh, 2013
6. Nicholls, Chater and Lask, 2000
7. Chatoor, 2002
8. Fisher *et al.*,2014
9. Note that a child can both not be taking in the level of nutrients recommended for their age *and* not have a measurable deficiency.

Chapter 34

1. Nwaru *et al.*, 2014
2. Johansson *et al.*, 2004
3. Nwaru *et al.*, 2014
4. Muraro *et al.*, 2014
5. Lomer, 2015
6. Zopf *et al.*, 2009
7. Lomer, 2015
8. Children's Food Trust, 2015a
9. Paul *et al.*, 2015

Chapter 35

1. Kenny *et al.*, 2015
2. Daniels and Mandell, 2014

3. Odar Stough *et al.*, 2015
4. Nadon *et al.*, 2011
5. Cermak, Curtin and Bandini, 2010

Chapter 36

1. Miller *et al.*, 2009
2. Ayres and Robbins, 2005, p.5
3. Ayres and Robbins, 2005, p.6
4. Zimmer *et al.*, 2012, p.1186
5. Nadon *et al.*, 2011
6. Farrow and Coulthard, 2012
7. Farrow and Coulthard, 2012

Chapter 37

1. Manno *et al.*, 2005, p.145
2. Brackett, 2016

Chapter 38

1. National Statistics, 2016
2. Stegenga *et al.*, 2014
3. Peeters *et al.*, 2003
4. HM Government, 2017
5. HM Government, 2017
6. Oliver via Huffpost, 2016, see https://www.youtube.com/watch?v=a_aidpc_3KI
7. Buck, 2016
8. See https://campaignresources.phe.gov.uk/resources/campaigns/17-change4life/overview
9. See www.henry.org.uk
10. See www.childfeedingguide.co.uk/common-feeding-pitfalls/restriction
11. Anderson and Keim, 2016
12. Blissett and Haycraft, 2008

Nurture Early Learning, New Zealand

1. See http://nurtureearlylearning.co.nz/nutrition-and-wellbeing

Index